ROBERT R.
Historic Hertfordshire
942.58 ROB.

9780900519017

Copy 1.

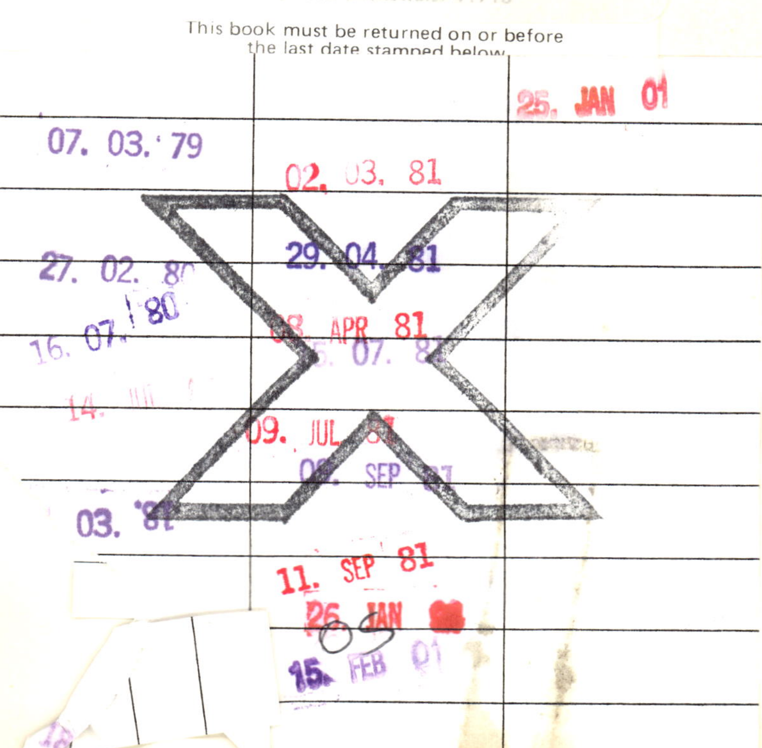

HISTORIC
HERTFORDSHIRE

RUDOLPH ROBERT

Published by
HERTFORDSHIRE COUNTRYSIDE

LETCHWORTH PRINTERS LTD.,
NORTON WAY NORTH, LETCHWORTH, HERTS

1968

CONTENTS

Chapter		Page
	Preface	9
1	Wheathampstead—stronghold of the Catuvellauni ...	11
2	Verulamium—the " rose-red city half as old as time "	16
3	Roman theatre	19
4	A museum of Roman antiquities	23
5	Benedictine abbey of St. Albans	26
6	The Peasants' Revolt	31
7	Wars of the Roses and battles long ago	35
8	Cottage homes	41
9	Fore Street and the Old Palace, Hatfield	44
10	Prisoner in the palace	48
11	Hatfield House and its art treasures	52
12	Amelia, the harum-scarum	56
13	The third Marquess of Salisbury, last of the eminent Victorians	59
14	Lemsford—the village with a song in its heart ...	64
15	The romance of William and Caroline Lamb ...	67
16	A bonfire of Byron's letters	71
17	Lord Melbourne, guide, philosopher and friend to Queen Victoria	76
18	Lord and Lady Palmerston, the lovers who married at fifty	80
19	Fun of the fair	85
20	The merry monarch and Nell Gwynne at Salisbury Hall	89
21	Hertford—the county town	94
22	Hertford Castle	98
23	Cromwell in Hertfordshire	103
24	Sir Hugh Myddleton and the New River	107
25	East India College, Haileybury	111
26	The story of Thomas Dimsdale	114
27	Samuel Whitbread—zealous advocate of the oppressed	117
28	Sporting inns	121
29	Diamond magnates at Tewin	124
30	Sir Ebenezer Howard and the new towns	128
31	A brief history of Digswell House	130

Chapter   Page
32 Welwyn Garden City   134
33 Brassey builds the viaduct   137
34 Holding fast the heritage   141
    Bibliography   143

LIST OF ILLUSTRATIONS

Between pages

Gaius Julius Cæsar (102–44 B.C.) — 32 and 33
St. Helen's church, Wheathampstead — ,,
Verulamium—student excavators — ,,
Morris dancers at Verulamium — ,,
Verulamium—the Roman theatre — ,,
The museum of Roman antiquities — ,,

Verulamium—model of the south-east (London) gate — 48 and 49
St. Albans abbey, and a fragment of the Roman wall — ,,
St. Albans abbey—the central tower — ,,
St. Albans—the great gateway — ,,
King Henry VIII, who dissolved the monasteries in 1543 — ,,
St. Albans—the war memorial and St. Peter's church — ,,

A Lemsford cottage — 64 and 65
A cottage home at Digswell — ,,
A cottage in old Hatfield — ,,
Hatfield—a Georgian-style doorway in Fore Street — ,,
Hatfield—Fore Street glimpsed through a picturesque arch — ,,
Hatfield—the Old Palace — ,,
Hatfield House—the south front — ,,
Queen Elizabeth I—the rainbow portrait — ,,
William Cecil, Lord Burghley — ,,
Hatfield House—the armoury — ,,
The statue of Lord Salisbury outside the gate of Hatfield House — ,,

Hatfield House—the west wing — 80 and 81
Robert Arthur Talbot Gascoyne Cecil, third Marquess of Salisbury — ,,
Hatfield—the church of St. Etheldreda — ,,
Lemsford village and the River Lea — ,,
Lemsford—a general view — ,,
Lemsford mill — ,,
Henry William Lamb, second Viscount Melbourne — ,,
Brocket Hall, acquired by Sir Matthew Lamb in 1746 — ,,
Brocket Park—sunshine among the trees — ,,
The lake in Brocket Park — ,,

	Between pages
Henry John Temple, third Viscount Palmerston	96 and 97
Brocket Park—two views of the Palladian bridge built by James Paine *c.* 1765	,,
Autumn in Brocket Park	,,
Fairground scenes at Welwyn Garden City	,,
King Charles II	,,
Nell Gwynne	,,
Salisbury Hall	,,
Nell Gwynne's cottage	,,
The County Hall, Hertford	,,
Hertford—the war memorial	112 and 113
Hertford Castle	,,
Hertford Castle—the Norman wall	,,
Hertford castle—the postern gate	,,
Hertford museum	,,
An old malting at Hertford	,,
Hertford—decorative plaster work on a shop front	,,
Oliver Cromwell	,,
Hertford—St. Andrew's church	,,
Great Amwell—the memorial to Sir Hugh Myddleton	,,
Samuel Whitbread	136 and 137
Essendon—the church of St. Mary	,,
Bedwell	,,
Tewin church	,,
The Fighting Cocks inn at St. Albans	,,
Tewin Water	,,
Digswell House	,,
Lombardy poplars in Welwyn Garden City	,,
Digswell viaduct	,,
Sir Ebenezer Howard	,,
New-town sculpture at Stevenage	,,

*The photographs, except where otherwise acknowledged,
are by the author.*

PREFACE

THOUGH the stories brought together between the covers of this book range over a period of 2,000 years, from Queen Boadicea to Queen Elizabeth II, they do not, of course, form a complete history of Hertfordshire, and are intended only as an introduction to a rich, varied and inexhaustible subject. For detailed studies about either the county as a whole or particular parts of it the reader is referred to lengthier and more learned works, such as the *Victoria County History*, to be found in the reference rooms of most public libraries. However, not everyone has time nowadays to delve deeply and trace in these works the full and fascinating record of times past.

The aim of *Historic Hertfordshire* is a modest one, to deal at reasonable length with some of the highlights of county history, particularly those more dramatic episodes that merge into the national history. In between are lighter pieces, of county interest only, and the choice of these has necessarily been somewhat arbitrary. The selected material and the collection of photographs will, it is hoped, interest both those who already know their Hertfordshire well and those who would like to know it better.

Acknowledgments are due to Mr. Leslie Bichener, editor of *Hertfordshire Countryside*, the county magazine, in which many of the stories and illustrations first appeared. It is also necessary to place on record my debt to the innumerable sources—books, newspapers, pamphlets—from which facts and information have been gleaned.

R. R.

CHAPTER ONE

WHEATHAMPSTEAD—STRONGHOLD OF THE CATUVELLAUNI

THERE are probably few villages in mid-Hertfordshire more tranquil than Wheathampstead or less affected by contemporary changes. To the visitor it appears little more than a long street running steeply downhill, a typical piece of old-style ribbon development—a straggle of houses and shops, a church with a fine spire, a wheelwright's yard, an old mill, a bridge spanning the River Lea, an historic inn and a disused railway station. The surrounding countryside bears, as yet, few signs of the industrial invasion so much in evidence in other parts of the county. New roads have brought a heavy increase of motor traffic, but despite this Wheathampstead manages to retain its character as a country village.

Surveying its modest rural charms on a summer evening, one gains the impression of a sleepy hamlet in which nothing of importance happens, or indeed has ever happened since time began. Certainly it is difficult to believe that one of the earliest battles of Britain was fought in the quiet fields in which the farmers now grow their wheat and barley. The history books do not say much about the battle, partly because its result was indecisive and partly because it took place at a time when many of our ancestors were still painting themselves with woad and living in wattle-and-daub huts.

The Belgic tribes

Before the Romans first set foot in Britain some 2,000 years ago much of south-eastern Hertfordshire, covered by dense and impenetrable forest, was of little use to the agriculturist. Elsewhere in the county, however, there was less woodland and the soil was ideal for the growing of corn. So it came about that the Belgic tribes who crossed the Channel about 200 B.C. settled down in Hertfordshire and in the counties adjoining it. South of the Lea the land was occupied by the Catuvellauni, an industrious and virile tribe that was later to throw up a remarkable leader. Wheathampstead, where the remnants of a defensive earthwork still exist, was in all probability this tribe's major settlement and stronghold.

For approximately 150 years the Catuvellauni dominated that part of Hertfordshire, wresting a bounteous living—even, it is believed, an exportable surplus—from the fertile corn belt. They were a turbulent people, constantly engaged in warlike operations against their neighbours (notably the Trinovantes, who lived in Essex) but by no means lacking in civilized virtues. In 55 B.C. news winged its way through the forest clearings to the *oppidum* at Wheathampstead that the famous Roman general Julius Cæsar, the conqueror of Gaul, had landed on England's south-east coast. As we now know, that was merely a reconnaissance, not a full-scale invasion. Cæsar, after penetrating some way inland, quickly withdrew, only to return in the following year with such a display of armed might that it obliged the Belgic tribes to cease their internecine warfare and band together in mutual defence. There was a meeting of the leaders at some unknown spot, and Cassivellaunus, head of the strong and energetic Catuvellauni tribe, was entrusted with command of the combined British forces. Preparations were made to resist the Roman legions and, if possible, drive them back into the sea.

Cæsar marches

Cæsar, with five legions (i.e. about 25,000 men), landed at Sandwich in July 54 B.C., and within a week had reached the Thames, on the northern bank of which the Britons had decided to make a stand. They were no match, however, for the heavily armed Roman troops, who forced their way across the river and broke through the defences. The exact route that Cæsar then took is uncertain, but it has been conjectured that the " track " which he mentions in *De Bello Gallico* may have followed the line of Watling Street. Cassivellaunus and his army were then falling back slowly, harassing the invaders, blocking their advance, and inflicting such casualties as they could.

Cæsar, of course, had many advantages over his opponent. The campaigns in Gaul had proved him a resolute commander and expert strategist. His troops, consisting mainly of heavy infantry, were highly disciplined and provided with all the accoutrements of war then available. Each legionary had his metal helmet, shield, cuirass and greaves. His personal fighting weapons were the sword and the *pilum*, or throwing spear. Supporting the infantry were the lighter-armed *velites*, the cavalry (2,000 strong), and possibly contingents of archers and slingers—altogether a formidable force. Organizationally, with their corps of centurions and subordinate officers, the legions were exceptionally strong.

Cassivellaunus, after failing to prevent the Thames crossing, must have realized that the odds were heavily against him, though his own army was of intimidating size. He had ample man-power, for the English countryside, despite its untamed character, bore a relatively high population. His Catuvellauni warriors, though inclined to unruliness, were tough and courageous. They had, moreover, the advantage of being familiar with the terrain over which they fought. Most important of all, they were more mobile than the Romans, for their chariots, which they handled with superb skill, gave them (as Cæsar himself admitted) the speed of cavalry and the power of infantry. At the same time they could be formidable enemies in fighting pitched battles on foot.

Nevertheless, the Roman superiority was such that by mid-August Cæsar had reached the Wheathampstead stronghold, into which the retreating Catuvellauni had retired for safety. Approximately 100 acres in extent, the *oppidum*—designed for exactly some such emergency as this—was well stocked with cattle, food and water supplies. The natural defences of woodland, marsh and scrub were massively augmented by earthworks and trenches, the dimensions of which excite wonder even today. The Romans, however, were past masters in the art of siege.

The assault

We may perhaps deduce the practical means adopted from those employed in Gaul, where Cæsar had learnt how to quell rebellious tribes and reduce fortified positions. Beleaguered towns had been surrounded by high ramparts and in some cases by movable towers, from which the defenders could be harried. Powerful siege works— the very sight of which could produce demoralization and panic— were then brought into action.

Whether anything like that happened at Wheathampstead, whether such standard engines of war as ballistæ or catapultæ were used, we can only guess. Writing in the *Commentaries*, Cæsar records briefly that the Catuvellauni were attacked from two sides, that they withstood the assaults bravely for some time but when the Roman infantry broke into the camp the tribesmen scattered and fled. " Many of the garrison," he concludes laconically, " were captured and killed."

Cassivellaunus was not himself at Wheathampstead during the siege. He had marched with a small " commando " band to the coast, where 800 Roman ships lay at anchor, in an attempt to destroy them and to create a diversion. Determined though it was, the raid on the fleet failed, and Cassivellaunus, deserted by the Trinovantes and other allies, had no alternative but to sue for peace. The victor, having demanded hostages and levied tribute, then moved back with his legions—not perhaps too satisfied with the outcome of the campaign, for the cost had been immense and the gains negligible. There was little to show in the way of loot or portable spoils. As for the tribute, Cæsar probably doubted whether, once he was on the other side of the Channel, it would ever be paid.

He set sail in mid-September, before the onset of the bad weather, and Britain saw little more of the Romans for 100 years.

The Devil's Dyke

There has been much learned debate as to the exact site of the British redoubt. Earthworks in Hertfordshire are by no means rare, and the battle may possibly have been fought at some other place. The *Victoria County History* (Vol. IV, published 1914) opts for Verulamium as being the only late Celtic stronghold answering to Cæsar's description. Certainly it was, like the *oppidum* at Wheathampstead, surrounded by woodland on three sides, while on the fourth side was marshy land. Verulamium, too, was defended by a rampart and ditch, and so, in the light of the evidence then available, it was reasonable to assume that the battle took place there.

However, extensive research work undertaken in the past fifty years runs counter to this conclusion. The long excavations at Verulamium have made it possible to piece together the city's history and prehistory with considerable accuracy. Expert opinion now inclines to the view that Wheathampstead was the scene of the battle. Mr. Philip Corder, in his monograph " Verulamium 1930-40 " (first published in *Antiquity* and later issued as a Veru-lamium Museum publication), discusses the earthworks in Prae Wood, near St. Albans, where abundant evidence of a Belgic occupation was found. He declares that careful study of a great mass of pottery made it possible to assign the occupation to the time of

Tasciovanus (the son of Cassivellaunus) and his successor. " This," concluded Mr. Corder, " ruled out entirely the traditional view that Verulamium was the stronghold of Cassivellaunus stormed by Julius Cæsar in 54 B.C." He goes on to say that investigations at Beach Bottom Dyke led to the great earthwork at Wheathampstead, some five miles distant.

Possibly, at some later date, further evidence—the skeleton of a Roman soldier, a battered helmet or a lost dispatch—may be forthcoming to settle the matter once and for all. Meantime we have the Devil's Dyke, on the eastern side of Wheathampstead, to assure us that the whole thing is not just a myth, a romantic legend of the countryside, or a well-worn tavern tale. The massive earthwork, now protected by the National Trust, is at one point over 100 feet wide and thirty-three feet deep.

Heavily overshadowed by trees, and steeped in perpetual gloom, it has an atmosphere of sinister foreboding. A first glimpse of it is apt to communicate a mysterious thrill, even though one knows nothing of its historical associations. When they are known imagination at once begins to stir. The uncanny silence that normally reigns in Devil's Dyke is broken by the clash of arms, by trumpet blasts that deafen the mind's ear, by the twanging of bowstrings, the neighing of horses, and harsh human cries. Savage men are glimpsed in the shadows; there are waving banners, dead bodies, and rivers of blood. One senses all the excitement, the heroism and the horror of that battle long ago.

CHAPTER TWO

VERULAMIUM—THE " ROSE-RED CITY HALF AS OLD AS TIME "

THE centre of modern St. Albans, with its buses, motor-cars and chain stores, is very much of the twentieth century. Only when the bustle and the market stalls of St. Peter's Street have been left behind, and our steps are turned in a westerly direction, does the atmosphere seem to change. Then the centuries, rich in historical associations, quickly roll back. By the time that we are in Fishpool Street, with its raised pavements, picturesque inns and half-timbered houses, the present has merged with the eighteenth century and the medieval past. Crossing the stone bridge over the tiny River Ver completes the illusion of remoteness in point of time, for on the other side we find ourselves among the scattered remains of a civilization that flourished 1,900 years ago.

The story of Verulamium, third largest city of Roman Britain, begins in A.D. 45, when the first buildings of wattle and daub rose from the fields on either side of Watling Street, the military high-way running from Dover to the north-west. Verulamium grew rapidly and was honoured by being granted the status of a *municipium*, the inhabitants of which enjoyed all the privileges of Roman citizenship.

Boadicea's revolt

This distinction was, however, to have dire results almost immediately afterwards, for in the surrounding countryside (densely afforested at that time) a strong " resistance movement " was developing against the invaders. The native Britons, groaning under an alien yoke, were already preparing to regain their independence, and in A.D. 61, under the leadership of Boadicea, they joined together in a powerful and widespread revolt which almost suc-ceeded in terminating the Roman rule and sending the legions back, in disorderly rout, to their continental bases. Incensed by the humiliations to which their queen had been subjected, the Iceni launched an overwhelming attack on the stronghold of Verulamium, which they sacked and burnt to the ground.

The Romans, and the Romanized citizens, were slaughtered in

16

a great carnage, and upwards of 70,000 people, irrespective of age or sex, perished in the city. Camulodunum (Colchester) and Londinium (London) had already been destroyed.

Flushed with these great victories, the army of Britons marched northward to meet the forces of Suetonius Paulinus, the Roman governor of Britain, and, on an unknown battlefield, lost all that they had gained. Peace was restored, and the city of Verulamium rose again from its blackened foundations, complete with a forum, an open-air theatre, temples and courts of justice, to live in comparative calm for many centuries. The wealthy, upper-class Romans built for themselves and their families villas with beautifully designed mosaic floors (several are to be seen in the Verulamium Museum), and with central heating systems of a type considered advanced even today. A dyke was dug and a wall constructed to guard this second city and its inhabitants from further attack.

Christian martyr

Verulamium prospered and then, according to the archæologists, in the third century A.D. a period of decay set in. Many of the architectural glories crumbled, and the buildings sank into a state of disrepair and ruin. The great days of Verulamium were over, and despite a brief " Constantian renaissance " its wealth and population gradually decreased until, in the fourth century, it lay derelict. By the time that the Romans withdrew from Britain the once proud, imperious city on the Ver was abandoned to criminals, outlaws and fugitives. Wolves and foxes roamed through the deserted streets.

A curtain comes down on the drama and does not really rise again until Offa, king of the Mercians, walks on to the stage of history. He saw, and marvelled at, the remains of the old pagan civilization, and (a practical man) decided to use Verulamium as a mine from which to hew the brick and stone with which to build a Benedictine monastery on Holmhurst Hill, on the other side of the river. The site was the one on which, according to tradition, Alban, a prominent citizen of Roman times, had been martyred for his Christian beliefs.

So began a process of demolition that was to extend over many subsequent centuries. Building materials were excavated from the " rose-red " city in ever-greater quantities, first by the Saxon and then by the Norman conquerors. The present abbey, whose massive

B

tower is so much admired for its dignity and strength, dates from shortly after the conquest of 1066. An impressive landmark, visible for miles around, it was built by abbot Paul de Caen, and can be seen to best advantage from a point within the boundaries of Verulamium—looking through a break in the Roman wall and across the lovely lake with its swans and wooded islands. The tower, on closer inspection, will be seen to consist of layer upon layer of brick toned to a mellow red by centuries of exposure to sun, wind and rain. There is something timeless and indestructible about the dour edifice. One hardly needs telling that the tower of St. Albans abbey is constructed of bricks taken by the Normans from Verulamium—*Roman* bricks—to form what is assuredly the most tangible and inspiring relic of the " forgotten city "; for such, after another 700 years of spoliation, it had become. By the eighteenth century nothing was left but a fragment here and there to testify to its former greatness. The vandals of " the age of reason," seeking materials with which to build new inns, houses and shops, made the last wholesale raids on Verulamium; cartloads of brick were taken away for the repair of the country roads. At last the quarry was exhausted.

Weeds and wild grasses

Britain's first-discovered Roman theatre was used by the townspeople of St. Albans as a rubbish tip. The gorgeous mosaic pavements and the foundations of the forum, the baths and the villas subsided beneath the soil. Verulamium was overgrown by weeds and wild grasses.

Not until the 1930s did a team of trained archæologists begin systematic excavations on the unique 200-acre site with a view to unearthing some of its buried treasures and secrets.

CHAPTER THREE

ROMAN THEATRE

WELL over a century has now elapsed since a St. Albans farmer found an ancient and long-buried ruin in the field he was ploughing. The site was close to the forum of the Roman city of Verulamium, and only a brief inspection, undertaken by a local archæologist, was needed to establish that the remains had historic value. They lay in the northern half of the city, in an area that dates back to the first century of the Christian era.

When the momentary stir of interest caused by the farmer's discovery had ended the matter was forgotten. Excavations, in fact, were not commenced until 1933, in which year the Earl of Verulum, owner of the field, provided funds for laying bare the foundations of what had been identified as a Roman theatre. Semi-circular in shape, it consisted, when built in the second century A.D., of an orchestra, a stage and a sloping bank of earth which supported rows of wooden seats. By piecing together the evidence provided by the stonework and by the pottery and coins discovered on the site, it has been possible to date and trace the history of the theatre, which at the time that the excavations were made was the only Roman theatre known to exist in this country.

The original building was probably erected between A.D. 140 and 150 and was of simple and orthodox design.

Development of the theatre

The orchestra was, as in the early Greek theatre, circular in shape and surrounding it almost completely was a massive earthwork or ramp, built up from the soil that was dug out of the interior. There may, when it was finished, have been a small, primitive type of stage, but it would appear that interest was mainly concentrated on the circular orchestra or arena. At a later period this emphasis was changed; the stage became of primary importance, and the orchestra was filled in, at least in part, with more wooden seats.

The floor of the stage, or *pulpitum*, was also of wood, the floor-boards being supported on uprights. Underneath the stage was a hollow or pit, the object of which is not definitely known; it may have served the dual purpose of draining away rain-water and improving acoustics. There was a room at the back of the stage for use by the actors.

This first rudimentary structure was altered, redesigned and improved upon as the public demand for entertainments increased. In what may be termed the second period of the theatre's existence the stage was greatly enlarged, and the appointments in general were of a sophisticated kind. Behind the stage rose the *scena*, richly ornamented with columns and statues, and with paintings that varied according to the type of play presented. The column shown in the photograph is a modern reconstruction, but the Corinthian capital by which it is surmounted is original. It was actually found in the theatre, together with an iron counterpoise that may have been used for raising and lowering a curtain.

According to the experts, the third century was a period of decline; the buildings were neglected and fell into a near-ruinous condition. When circumstances changed again, and interest in the theatre revived, a complete reconstruction had to be undertaken. The stage wings were rebuilt on new lines; additions were made to the structure, including perhaps a tiled roof; the seating capacity was increased; and a triumphal arch was erected. Everything points to the conclusion that in this final phase the theatre reached the zenith of its fame and popularity.

The entertainments

How such a grandiose playhouse was kept going—whether by private or municipal enterprise—is a matter for speculation. Conjectural, too, are the types of play, the spectacles and interludes provided to make a Romano-British holiday. We can only assume that they were similar to those of the capital city, Rome, which set the fashion in amusements as in everything else.

The early Roman theatre was modelled on the Greek theatre, but differed from it in one important respect: there was no close and intimate link with religion. This inevitably affected play production, and indeed the whole nature of the uses to which the theatre was put. Where the great Greek dramatists—Aeschylus, Euripedes and Sophocles—excelled in tragic masterpieces that involved the gods and mythical heroes, the Roman playwrights were at their best in comedies that dealt with human beings and their actions. While, therefore, we cannot rule out the possibility that *Agamemnon*, *Medea* and *Oedipus Rex* were performed at Verulamium it is probable that interpretations of contemporary life, exposures of the follies of ordinary people and stories with happy endings were most in favour. Comedy, at first inspired by the Greek Menander, was the Roman forte. Such tragedies as they produced were not of enduring quality and, in fact, very few have survived.

Among the most popular Roman dramatists was Plautus (*c.* 254-184 B.C.), an Umbrian who settled in Rome and was a baker before turning his hand to the writing of plays. Working with tireless industry, he produced over fifty comedies, based on Greek originals, and about twenty of them have survived to the present day. Another distinguished, though less prolific, playwright was Terence, (*c.* 190-159 B.C.)—brought to Rome as a Carthaginian slave. Six of his comedies have come down to us and are notable for their subtle character studies. That these two famous playwrights —Plautus and Terence—were given a hearing at Verulamium seems reasonably certain. There must, of course, have been hundreds of others—some of them, possibly, native Britons—whose wit and wisdom delighted whole generations of playgoers but of whom we know nothing.

A third kind of dramatic entertainment that seems to have held the Roman stage was pantomime—the dumb show in which the actors told their story entirely by gestures, facial expression and dancing. No doubt the Verulamium audiences were also given displays by trapeze artists, jugglers and acrobats. When plays became tedious the producers recaptured the interest of their audiences by staging triumphal processions, battle scenes and similar spectacles. Music, when demanded, was supplied by flautists and a group of singers—the chorus.

These were the orthodox, polite forms of entertainment; but the Romans had a taste for cruelty in the theatre. It was quite a common practice to scourge convicted criminals and torment wild beasts on the stage. Pliny records, for example, that at the opening of Pompey's theatre in ancient Rome 500 lions and twenty elephants were slaughtered. In the Colosseum (which is an amphitheatre or " double theatre ") Christians were thrown to the lions, prisoners of war were made to fight to the death, and gladiators engaged in brutal combats with sword and trident.

The theatre at Verulamium was small by comparison with the theatres of Rome, some of which held upwards of 40,000 spectators, but it would be sentimental to assume that blood never flowed there. At the very least there will have been trials of human strength, wrestling, minor gladiatorial contests and the killing of animals, for all these things were part of the Roman way of life.

Buried in the fields

As the fifth century dawned, Verulamium's theatre had not only lost importance but was again falling into a state of decay. When the Roman occupation of Britain ended in A.D. 407, and later, when the Saxons came, the process of active demolition began. Building materials of all kinds were hewn from the crumbling city as from a quarry. The massive outer walls of the theatre were knocked down for the bricks they contained, and once they had gone the ramp of earth with its rising tiers of seats gradually collapsed. Then, when the theatre was no more than a hollow in the ground, it became a dump for vegetable refuse and household rubbish. At last, the vandals having done their worst, it disappeared completely from view, and lay buried in the fields by the side of Watling Street, the Roman highway that ran north from Dover to Chester—hidden until the day of its accidental rediscovery in the nineteenth century.

Excavations were begun in 1933, and among the refuse and debris were found 3,000 Roman coins, a great deal of pottery and many animal bones, chiefly those of sheep and oxen. Some of these interesting relics may be seen in the nearby Verulamium Museum, which was built for the sole purpose of housing the Roman antiquities.

Other Roman theatres, it must be mentioned, have been identified in recent years at Canterbury and Colchester, so Verulamium can no longer claim to have the only known Roman theatre in the country, or even the oldest, but it certainly was the first to be found, excavated and made visible.

CHAPTER FOUR

A MUSEUM OF ROMAN ANTIQUITIES

EXCAVATIONS on the Roman city of Verulamium began, in a tentative way, in 1847 after a farmer had drawn attention to crumbling masonry in a field. A local antiquary who made investigations identified the Roman theatre, at that time the only one known in this country. Many years later, in 1953, the Earl of Verulam, owner of the site, was approached, and not only gave permission for excavation but generously provided funds. The original building of the theatre, the eastern façade of which fronted on to Watling Street, belongs to the second century of the Christian era. In the process of digging, coins, broken pottery, animal bones and part of what is believed to have been a curtain-raising apparatus were found.

Just before the start of the work on the theatre a team of archæologists had begun systematic excavation in another part of the Verulamium site. Between 1930 and 1939, as means became available and opportunity offered, a large area in the southern portion of the city was cleared, and cuttings were made across the former defences. The most important of these excavations, made between 1930 and 1934, were under the direction of Sir Mortimer Wheeler and the late Mrs. Tessa Verney Wheeler, and resulted in a number of valuable finds.

Eventually so many objects of interest accumulated that the question of housing and exhibiting them arose.

City council aid

Plans for a Verulamium museum were then considered. In May 1939, when the building was complete, the Earl of Harewood formally opened it to the public. The museum, erected at the cost of St. Albans City Council, attracted widespread attention, and is now regarded as one of the best of its kind to be found in the country.

Within its walls the story of Verulamium is unfolded in a series of displays, in specimens, models and pictures. Visitors will find a plan of the Roman city, and detailed guide books to the excavations and finds. In the annex to the museum is an interesting hypocaust, part of a domestic bath suite which, nearly 2,000 years ago, was used by the owner of a large villa. The tessellated pavement above the heating ducts is virtually intact, and has exceptional interest.

St. Albans City Council, which, as mentioned above, bore the entire cost of building the museum, authorized further expenditure in 1958 amounting to £22,000 for extending the museum, so that many important new finds could be properly housed. In further proof of the council's enlightened concern for the " little Pompeii " on its doorstep may be mentioned the fact that an annual grant is made to the committee responsible for excavations. Much help is also given—mainly through the city engineer and surveyor's department—in the form of advice, the loan of tools and the provision of labour.

Discoveries 1955-9

During World War II, and for some years after, little work was done on the Verulamium site, but in 1955 a road-widening scheme, involving part of the Roman city, started off a fresh series of excavations. The foundations of shops and houses were revealed, and evidence came to light which suggested that some of the earlier conclusions regarding the date of the walls and the length of time that Verulamium was inhabited would have to be revised.

Among the Roman shops was one which, judging from the amphora shards found, belonged to a wine-seller. Carpenters' tools —hammers, chisels and a plane—were dug up from another. A third was a bronze-worker's shop, probably supplying saucepans, frying pans and similar utensils to citizens. Of little intrinsic value, such articles can yet add significantly to our knowledge of a period.

A more important find of the 1959 season was a yellow plaster frieze, ornamented with a scroll design, which had collapsed on the floor of a Roman house. This frieze, when recovered and restored, was first exhibited at the British Museum, and attracted much attention both from experts and from the general public. Another much-admired discovery was a ten-inch-high statuette, identified as a Venus—a figurine that might have stood in the shrine of a private house. How it came to be in the bronzesmith's workroom is a matter of pure speculation.

At about the same time a mosaic pavement of exceptionally fine workmanship was uncovered—in the same house that had yielded up the plaster frieze. The mosaic, which probably dates back to the second century, is noteworthy for its fine central panel, which depicts, in realistic style and great detail, a lion dragging off a deer. Archæologists regard this pavement as one of the most exciting Roman finds in the whole of Britain for many years.

Lifting operations

After the " lion mosaic " was unearthed in 1959 it was bedded down again to protect it against damp and frost. During the excavating season of 1960 it was again uncovered, and plaster which had collapsed on it was removed; then once again the pavement was covered with straw and soil. Throughout the whole of 1961, while building work on the Verulamium museum was in progress, it lay undisturbed. When the extension was completed, early in 1962, Dr. I. E. Anthony, the museum director, at once began arranging the new material with a view to having the gallery open for the Easter holiday.

The " lion mosaic," eagerly awaited, could not, however, be lifted until late May, when the better weather conditions had arrived and the pavement—which had been covered by more than a foot of snow in January—was thoroughly dry. The work was given to the sons of Italian experts who had been responsible for mounting the Roman floors on show in the museum since pre-war days. Very great care had to be taken.

The twelve-foot-long pavement is now one of the principal and most admired exhibits in the new museum gallery.

CHAPTER FIVE

BENEDICTINE ABBEY OF ST ALBANS

ON a memorable day in A.D. 793, Offa, king of the Mercians, in the presence of a great gathering of Saxon kings, archbishops, bishops and other notables, laid the foundations of a Benedictine monastery on the brow of a Hertfordshire hill. The site was that on which the martyrdom of St. Alban had taken place in the days of the Roman occupation, when Christianity was a proscribed faith. Someone, digging in the flinty soil, had actually discovered the bones of the saint, and round them, at Offa's behest, there gradually arose a great complex of monastic buildings. Much of the brick and stone was quarried from the pagan city of Verulamium, which lay ruined and desolate just across the river.

When the Normans came the present cathedral was built, and the massive tower of weathered Roman brick, which is their handiwork, still remains—an enduring landmark visible for miles around. The first abbot—a friend of William the Conqueror—was Paul de Caen, a learned man, " rigid and prudent in the observance of the religious order," who kept control of the abbey for sixteen years. To prehistoric Prae Wood and Roman Verulamium was then added the city of St. Albans—for houses, workshops and civic buildings quickly sprang up in the shadow of the great Norman edifice.

The monastic appointments followed a well-established architectural plan. Adjoining the abbey, on the south side, were cloisters (traces of which may still be seen), a chapel, a dormitory, an infirmary and a garden. Beyond, on the slope of the hill, was another group of buildings which contained a chapter house, a common room, a refectory, granaries, a kitchen and a larder. There was also a block, with an audience chamber and royal apartments, for the use of distinguished visitors. A bakehouse, a brewhouse and a buttery provided the community with most of its requirements in the way of food and drink. Finally, there was accommodation within the monastery for guests and travellers, and stabling for 200 horses.

Life for the monks was a round, not perhaps too austere, of work, prayer and study. They practised the handicrafts, founded one of the earliest schools of painting in the country, developed the arts of music and mathematics, wrote books and built up a great library. As a result St. Albans achieved wide renown in medieval times as a centre of learning.

At least one name survives from those far-off days—that of Matthew Paris, who entered the monastery in 1217 and is chiefly remembered as an historian; but he also was a painter and a man of affairs. Indeed, so varied were his accomplishments in the fields of scholarship, diplomacy and art that it led to his being described as a " universal genius."

The Peasants' Revolt

During the 200 or 300 years that followed the Norman Conquest St. Albans grew in size and importance, and at the Council of Tours the abbey was recognized as the foremost in the country. Left undisturbed in their labours and meditations through decades of comparative calm and tranquillity, the monks prospered.

Then, in 1349, a great calamity broke up the long peace. The Black Death came to St. Albans and roamed the streets at will, taking impartial toll of rich and poor, godly and ungodly. Many of the monks and the abbot of that time fell victim to the pestilence. Nor were the villages in the surrounding countryside spared. There, as elsewhere, the Black Death created havoc, and soon, because of the large numbers of peasants who died, agricultural work came to a virtual standstill.

Within a year foodstuffs doubled in price, and such labourers as remained demanded big wage increases. To this the landowners replied by forcing Parliament to pass the Statute of Labourers, which compelled all able-bodied unemployed under sixty to work for anyone who might so require. A labourer leaving his work could be imprisoned, and the statute expressly decreed that " the old wages and no more shall be given to servants." When, in addition to these harsh measures, an unpopular poll tax was imposed the peasant mass rose in a nation-wide movement of revolt.

Chauncy, the Hertfordshire historian, tells us that in 1384 Wat Tyler and Jack Straw " with an army of rebels " marched to St. Albans and demanded of the abbot, Thomas de la Mare, that he hand to them the various charters that made them serfs. Much of the demonstrating by the peasants was done outside the great gateway which formed the main entrance to the monastery and is the only part of it still standing.

There may have been behind the monastery walls men who realized that the peasants had a just cause; but they were powerless, and could do nothing but look out from their stronghold on the sea of impassioned faces and wonder what would happen next. Suddenly it was rumoured that Wat Tyler had been killed, and the drama then moved to its inevitable close. Richard II, with armoured knights and archers, moved on St. Albans and subdued the rebels. John Ball and fifteen Hertfordshire men were dragged to an open space near the great gateway and executed. Their dream of an England in which there would be " neither gentlemen nor villeins " faded, and the besieged monastery returned to its normal way of life.

The Reformation

At the beginning of the fourteenth century the Benedictines were at the very height of their prosperity. They owned extensive lands, they ran industries and handicrafts, they were the repositories of culture and the dispensers of charity to the poor. As their wealth and authority increased it was perhaps inevitable that the medieval monarchs and nobles, often hard pressed for money with which to wage war and indulge their extravagant tastes, should feel envious. The coming of the Reformation to England in the sixteenth century gave them their pretext for open confiscation of the ecclesiastical properties.

Henry VIII is, of course, the central figure of the great upheaval which culminated in the dissolution of the monasteries and led, as at St. Albans, to their virtual destruction. This improvident monarch, having first squandered a great fortune left him by his father, Henry VII, and then debased the coinage, was faced with many and diverse troubles. His marriage to Anne Boleyn after the divorce from Catherine of Aragon had already resulted in a breach with Rome, and subsequent events quickly worsened the position. In 1535 the smaller monasteries with less than £200 a year were compulsorily closed. Between 1536 and 1539 the larger ones were given the alternative of voluntary or forced surrender. In 1540 the operation was concluded by an Act of Parliament which transferred the expropriated properties to the Crown, whose revenues were then doubled.

Henry assumed the title of " Supreme head of the Church of

England," and declared himself, by virtue of his kingship, " God's vicar on earth." All authority was taken from the Catholic Church and the dispossessed monks, abbots and priors were compensated by grants of small pensions. On the other hand, leading ministers and courtiers were rewarded for their support by extravagant grants of free land.

Richard Boreman de Stevenache, the last abbot of St. Albans, must have been in pensive mood when, on December 5, 1539, he was obliged to make the act of submission to Sir Thomas Pope and other representatives of the king. It may be said that when the seals passed from his hands St. Albans moved from the medieval into the modern era. Henry made a grant of the abbey to Sir Richard Lee, and for about eleven years local builders used it as a quarry. Eventually, when the magnificent tower was on the point of being undermined, the townspeople stepped in and purchased the ruins for a few hundred pounds. The abbey then became the parish church and long afterwards, in 1877, St. Albans cathedral.

Points of interest

Few people like the west front, which is nineteenth-century Gothic, nor can it be said that the long nave is architecturally inspiring—though on the north side are several of the original Norman pillars.

Truly impressive, however, is the area of the central tower and the transepts, parts of which date back 900 years. Much of the work here is that of the first abbot, Paul de Caen; the massive pillars and arches, rough-hewn and primitive in their effect, are immensely strong. St. Alban's shrine and the watching gallery are at the very heart of the ancient fabric. Here was the goal of the long processions of pilgrims who came in medieval times from all over the country to view the saintly relics. The high screen, the tomb of Humphrey, Duke of Gloucester, and abbot John of Wheathampstead's chapel are other points of interest.

The fine painting in the south transept is by the Hertfordshire artist Frank Salisbury, and depicts the cortège of Queen Eleanor, consort of Edward I, on its way from Nottingham to Westminster, resting at St. Albans for the night. The monarch is shown seated on a black-caparisoned charger, surrounded by groups of red-robed monks and torch-bearers whose flares illuminate the calm features of the queen. Frank Salisbury's panel, which measures fifteen feet by five feet, marvellously re-creates the medieval atmosphere, and the colours glow with rich warmth against the austere stone.

There was a time, it should be remembered, when the entire abbey interior was one gorgeous fantasia of colour. The Benedictines were generous patrons of art, and employed craftsmen to decorate the walls and ceilings of their sacred edifice. In their day the white marble shrine of St. Alban glittered under a rich ornamentation of gold, silver and precious stones.

CHAPTER SIX

THE PEASANTS' REVOLT

EVER since Neolithic times Hertfordshire has been an important agricultural county. It was so in the era of Cassivellaunus and the Belgic tribes, through all the years of the Roman occupation and through the Middle Ages, and it continues to be so today. The fields that surround our thriving towns and villages have been cultivated by the men of countless past generations. Wheat and other corn crops have been grown on Hertfordshire's hill slopes and the banks of its rivers have watered the roots of orchards and vineyards since the dawn of civilization.

The whole pageant of Hertfordshire history, in fact, is to be seen moving against a background of glebeland and common, of arable and pasture, and the predominant figure in that pageant is the peasant. He it was who supported on his broad back the whole structure of society, toiling from dawn till sunset with a dour strength and patience. His whole existence circumscribed, monotonous and brutish, he was a long-suffering individual and not easily roused, but on at least one occasion he was provoked into making a desperate bid for release from the chains that bound him to the manor and to the soil on which he was born.

The story begins in 1349, the year in which the Black Death struck at St. Albans and other populated areas.

The Statute of Labourers

A particularly heavy toll was taken in St. Albans, not only of the townspeople but of the monks in the great Benedictine abbey, which was one of the centres of medieval learning, and the abbot himself was carried off by the pestilence.

The villages and hamlets of Hertfordshire enjoyed a brief immunity, and then they too were involved in the common disaster. The infection spread, and suddenly work on the scattered manors came to a standstill because of a total insufficiency of labourers. The Black Death had decimated their ranks.

Economic laws operated then very much as they do now, and within a year foodstuffs and other necessities had doubled in price.

The peasants, depleted in numbers as they were, not unnaturally demanded that their wages be increased, and this demand they were successful in enforcing.

Thereupon the landowners, acting through the Parliament of 1350, which they dominated, passed a Statute of Labourers, the effect of which was to compel all able-bodied persons under sixty not having the wherewithal to live to work for anyone who might require them to do so, with imprisonment as the penalty for refusal. A labourer leaving his work was to be regarded as a criminal, and the statute further decreed that " the old wages and no more shall be given to servants."

This law, as may well be imagined, caused great resentment, and it required only a spark to touch off the great historic event known as the Peasants' Revolt. That spark was the imposition of an unpopular poll tax.

The revolt, as we know, was of a nation-wide character, but reached its peak points in the south-eastern parts of the country. Delving into Sir Henry Chauncy's *History of Hertfordshire* for information, we read that " Wat Tyler and Jack Straw raised a great commotion in several counties " and that, in particular, they harried the abbot of St. Albans, Thomas de la Mare, with demands that he hand over to them the various charters that defined and restricted their liberties. Wat Tyler, marching on London, went even farther by presenting Richard II with claims that included the total and final abolition of serfdom and the commutation of all feudal service.

In Hertfordshire, as Chauncy tells us, " a great rabble gathered about the abbey gateway in St. Albans," with such demonstrations of hostility that the prior and a number of the monks fled for their lives. Standing in modern Romeland, it is easy to picture the scene with its horde of angry labourers, brandishing sticks and staves and truly formidable in their determination not to return to their villages and their tasks until their requests for freedom had been granted.

A wicked priest

After a while there came to St. Albans a rumour that the revolt in London had collapsed and that Wat Tyler, its leader, had been treacherously stabbed and was dead. On hearing this the Hertfordshire peasants were thrown into a state of confusion and became more moderate in their actions. Nevertheless, they continued

Gaius Julius Caesar (102-44 B.C.), Roman statesman and general, who in 55 B.C. crossed into Britain, repeating his visit in the following year.

H.H.—1

The church of St. Helen, Wheathampstead, stands in the middle of the village. Parts of the present building date back to the thirteenth century. The tower is surmounted by a leaden broach-spire, renewed just over a century ago. Old foundations indicate that there may have been a church on the site in Saxon days. A Roman road ran nearby.

The Roman theatre, Verulamium, as it is today. Though the column is modern the capital crowning it is original. Gladiatorial combats may have taken place in the small arena.

Verulamium. Student excavators at work on the foundations of a Roman building not far from the theatre.

The Verulamium museum, in which many of the most important Roman discoveries are housed.

Verulamium museum—an interior view. In the foreground is a model of the south-east (London) gate of Verulamium. Two of the mosaics discovered on the site can be seen in the background.

doggedly to insist that Abbot de la Mare should discharge them of all accustomed services and labours, and that the centuries-old yoke should be lifted from their necks.

" We are all come," they argued reasonably enough, " from one father and mother, Adam and Eve. How can the gentry show that they are greater lords than we? Yet they make us labour for their pleasure."

Unfortunately for them, the revolt had suffered a reverse from which it was impossible to recover. Wat Tyler had indeed been struck down—by the dagger of Sir William Walworth—and presently King Richard, having already " pacified " Essex and Kent, entered St. Albans with a great number of armed men and archers to quell the rebellion there.

A batch of prisoners was brought from Hertford to stand trial— among them being a " wicked priest," as Chauncy puts it, who had declared passionately that " things will never go well in England so long as goods be not in common, and so long as there be gentle-men and villeins."

This was none other than John Ball, an expounder of the doctrines of John Wyclif and a man who had become famous as a preacher. His forthright insistence on the principle of social equality had, however, caused him to be excommunicated and thrown into prison.

Executions

The part he played in the revolt was all-important: he had been its most eloquent and fearless advocate, and now, in the shadow of the abbey tower, he was called upon to pay the penalty. His captors gave him short shrift, and he was condemned to be hanged, drawn and quartered. On July 15, 1381, that barbaric sentence was carried out in the presence of the king. Then, immediately after " justice " had been done, the four quarters were rushed from St. Albans to be exhibited in other towns as a grisly warning to the disaffected. Fifteen men of the county were executed on the same day as the rebel priest.

The rising was crushed. " Serfs you were and serfs you will remain " boasted the king, whose handling of the revolt was marked by a complete lack of understanding and much brutality. However, the last word was not with him, but with the slow working of the historical process. The storming of the great gateway, still standing

C

a little to the west of the abbey, was not entirely in vain. The villeins gradually won their emancipation from the fetters of feudalism and, though they still had to endure many hardships, at last began to breathe freedom's air.

CHAPTER SEVEN

THE WARS OF THE ROSES AND BATTLES LONG AGO

" In this Countie at three severall times, three mortall and bloody Battels of England . . . have bene fought. The first whereof chaunced the 23 of Maye Anno 1455, in the towne of St. Albans by Richard Duke of York, with his associates, the Earls of Warwick and Sales-bury, and the Lords fawconbridge and Cobham, against King Henry VI, in whose defence Edmund Duke of Somerset, Henry Earl of Northumberland and John Lord Clifford . . . lost their lives. The second Battel likewise was fought in the towne of St. Albans . . . the 17 of February being Shrove Tuesday Anno 1461. . . . The third and last Battel was fought nere unto the towne of High Barnet upon the 14 of Aprill being Easter daye . . . Anno 1471."—JOHN SPEEDE.

THE Wars of the Roses, in which Hertfordshire played such a prominent part, were basically a dynastic struggle. Rival claimants to the throne of England, the Lancastrians and Yorkists, fought out their differences in a series of political and military conflicts that, from first to last, plagued the country for more than thirty yeras.

Henry IV established the house of Lancaster in 1399 by deposing his unlucky cousin Richard II, but had to deal during his short reign with one rebellion after another. Henry IV was succeeded by Henry V, the hero of Agincourt, who in turn passed on the crown to Henry VI, around whose person the wars revolved. Only an infant at the time of his accession, the king did not take after his warrior-father but developed into a man of peace and piety.

On coming of age in 1442 he aligned himself with the nobles who were opposed to continuing the war in France, which was going badly. The " hawks," however, were very strong, and so the impossible efforts to hold the conquered territories across the Channel continued. When failure resulted, the unhappy monarch and all those most closely associated with him became so unpopular that

Richard, Duke of York, found it an opportune moment to raise the banner of revolt.

First battle of St. Albans

Having raised an army on the border of Wales, he marched southward in the direction of London, accompanied by the Earls of Salisbury and Warwick, Lord Cobham, and other adherents. The king, having heard of these moves, rallied his own supporters —among them the Dukes of Somerset and Buckingham, the Earls of Pembroke and Stafford, and Lord Clifford—and moved northward from Westminster to meet the rebels. He spent the night at Watford, and on the following day, May 21, 1455, reached St. Albans, where he planted his standard in St. Peter's Street, now a busy shopping centre.

The king, according to the account given in Clutterbuck's *History of Hertfordshire*, entrusted the defences of the town to Lord Clifford and awaited the arrival of the insurgents. In fact, the duke and his forces were already encamped in a field called Key Field, to the south-east of St. Albans, and when Henry heard of this he sent the Duke of Buckingham to demand of the Yorkists whether the cause of their coming was peaceable or hostile. Their reply was to the effect that they intended no harm to the king but were his " true lieges," and would be satisfied by the delivery into their hands of the Duke of Somerset, " the traitor who lost Normandy, neglected the defence of Gascony, and brought the kingdom to its present unhappy state." This ultimatum the king was, naturally, unable to accept, and since further parleying proved fruitless the duke decided to resolve the issue by force.

The royal standard, as we have seen, was planted in St. Peter's Street, and it was there that the historic first battle of St. Albans was fought. Six hundred Yorkists under Sir Robert Ogle marched boldly from Key Field into the market place, and took the Lancastrians completely by surprise. The curfew bell on the clock tower was rung to sound the alarm, and the king's men, hurriedly getting into their harness, prepared to repel the attack. Though the struggle that ensued lasted no more than half an hour it was, in the words of map-maker John Speede, " mortall and bloody."

Gunpowder and cannon had been in general use all over Europe for more than a century, yet this battle between the white and red roses appears to have been fought in the main with swords and daggers. Men confronted one another face to face in a multitude of individual combats, every one of which had to be decided by physical strength and valour. Quarter being neither asked for nor given, St. Peter's Street was, within minutes, full of dead and dying. At last fortune favoured the numerically superior side—i.e. the Yorkists, who had some 3,000 troopers as against the king's estimated 2,000. Sheer weight broke the lines of the Lancastrians, who fled precipitately and sought shelter in nearby gardens and thickets.

Henry VI himself, wounded in the neck by an arrow, took refuge in a cottage, and remained there, abandoned by his followers, until discovered by the victorious Duke Richard, who conducted him to the abbey, where, before being escorted back to London, he was allowed to rest.

Later, at the intercession of the abbot, John of Wheathampstead, the corpses were removed from the streets and arrangements made for their decent burial. Eight hundred of the king's men, including the Duke of Somerset, and 600 of the Yorkists were killed—a total of approximately one quarter of those engaged on both sides. The seriously wounded, whose numbers must also have been considerable, found their way into religious and secular houses in the surrounding countryside.

For all its horror, this battle was no more than the prelude to a veritable war of extermination among the nobles, who when they were not fighting resorted to litigation, intrigue, terror and assassination to gain their ends. After the events of 1455 in St. Albans a compromise between the two rival houses was arranged, but the fundamental enmities continued smouldering beneath the surface, and it was not long before war broke out again.

The second battle of St. Albans

On Shrove Tuesday, February 17, 1461, the contending parties clashed for the second time in the streets and outskirts of St. Albans. On the Lancastrian side was Margaret of Anjou, Queen of Henry VI, and on the Yorkist side Richard Nevill, Earl of Warwick, whose role as " king-maker " has given him a permanent place in our history. Henry VI was, on the day of the battle, virtually his prisoner.

Margaret, who had gained a decisive victory at Wakefield, Yorkshire (where Duke Richard had been killed), was no doubt in optimistic mood as she and her army encamped at Barnard's Heath on a day normally given over to the making of confessions and pancakes. Her position was to the north of the town, and when news presently came that Warwick and the Yorkist army were approaching from the south she at once took the initiative and attacked.

The Lancastrians swept unopposed through St. Peter's Street, but met with strong and unexpected resistance by the cross in the market place, where a company of archers had been stationed. Warwick counter-attacked with great vigour, and the fighting went on for some time without either side being able to gain a clear advantage. At last the king-maker, inadequately supported by his reserves, had to fall back. Margaret, whose overriding ambition in life was to ensure the succession of her son Edward, redoubled her efforts, with the result that the Yorkists were utterly routed. Some 2,000 or 3,000 men, it is believed, were left dead on the field of battle. Many of them were buried in the churchyard of St. Peter's, in a mass grave.

Henry VI, who had been abandoned by the Lancastrians in the first battle at St. Albans, now found himself deserted by the Yorkists and was thus restored, unharmed, to his wife and the members of his own party. He still remained, poor man, the victim of a mental disorder and therefore a puppet, always at the mercy of other people.

After this notable Lancastrian victory the king, the queen, Prince Edward, and many of their attendant lords, repaired to the abbey for a thanksgiving service. The monks received their royal guests with appropriate ceremonies and conducted them to the altar. Later the abbot implored that the Lancastrian troops should be restrained from plundering the town, which, under their agreement with Margaret, they were entitled to do. She seems to have thought better of her decision, and a proclamation was issued calling upon the soldiers to refrain from acts of violence and looting. This appeal seems to have had little effect, and the townspeople must have heaved a sigh of relief when, after several days of turbulence, the army hurriedly moved out.

At Towton in March 1461 the Lancastrians' hard-won victory in Hertfordshire was reversed.

The battle of Barnet

Fought in a snowstorm, the battle of Towton resulted in the establishment of Edward, Duke of York, on the throne in place of

Henry VI, and brought the first phase of the wars to an end. Ten years later, when the Lancastrians had recovered their strength and conviction, there was a resumption of hostilities. Warwick the king-maker, after quarrelling with Edward IV, had changed sides, restored Henry VI to the throne, and become the white-rose leader. On April 14, 1471, he and Edward clashed at Barnet in a great battle to settle the bitter dispute as to who was best fitted to govern the country.

Warwick, accompanied by his brother, John Nevill the Marquis of Montacute, and by the Dukes of Exeter and Somerset and the Earl of Oxford, was the first to arrive upon the scene. Having assembled an army in the Midlands, he had passed through St. Albans and made his encampment at Gladmore Heath, about a mile to the north-west of Barnet, just as night was falling. The temporarily deposed king, Edward IV, coming with his army from London, arrived within a short distance of Warwick only a few hours later.

Early next morning, on Easter Day, when fully aware of one another's presence, there was a great blaring of trumpets and unfurling of banners on both sides. The leaders marshalled their forces in battle array, waited just long enough to allow the mists on the heath to disperse, and gave their orders for the fighting to begin.

" Never," says Clutterbuck, " were chieftains animated with more ferocious hatred of one another." His brief account makes it clear that, whatever may have happened at the two battles of St. Albans, artillery was used at Barnet—though only, apparently, in the opening stages. After a few salvoes the combatants advanced and became inextricably mixed on the field. Finally, after a merciless hand-to-hand struggle, the king's forces began to prevail, and those of Warwick, despite the inspiring example he himself set, to fall back. In a last-minute attempt to rally his men the king-maker, who certainly did not lack courage, rushed with raised sword and defiant cries into the Yorkist ranks. No one followed him, however, except his own brother, Montacute, and both were immediately hacked to death. The Lancastrian troops thereupon gave way on all sides and the day ended in an overwhelming Yorkist victory.

Ten thousand men, it has been estimated, were killed in this obstinately fought and terrible battle.

The roses unite

Still the Wars of the Roses dragged on. After Barnet, in May
1471, the contending parties fought yet again at Tewkesbury in
Gloucestershire—in the " Bloody Meadow " on the banks of the
Avon—and again the Lancastrians were routed. An uneasy peace
then reigned in the land for over a decade. Edward IV was succeeded by Edward V, and Edward V by Richard III—" Crouch-
back," suspected murderer of the two princes and usurper of the
throne.

The final chapter was not written until 1485, when Henry, Earl
of Richmond, raised a rebellion against the unpopular king. They
met at Bosworth Field and there, with the death of Richard, the
fratricidal strife that had disturbed the peace of the realm for over
thirty years ended. The new king, Henry VII, first of the Tudor
line, was the son of a Lancastrian heiress. When he married Elizabeth of York, Edward IV's eldest daughter, the two houses were
united and England moved out of the Middle Ages, with their
costly feuds and rivalries, into the dawn of a new and more settled
era.

CHAPTER EIGHT

COTTAGE HOMES

THERE is a certain magic about the word " cottage "—especially for townspeople, in whom it immediately conjures up visions of thatched roofs, dormer windows, and roses round the door. An unpretentious word, meaning simply " small country dwelling," it has become—through the influence of story, verse and song—a synonym for " bliss." John Collins, whose poem " Tomorrow " appears in Palgrave's *Golden Treasury*, may have started it all. His verses embody the dream of a happy old age in a cottage by the sea—

> " *With a porch at my door for both shelter and shade*
> *And a small plot of ground for the use of the spade.*"

For company he envisaged a " shambling pad pony," a cow, a dog, and a babbling brook that was to lull him to sleep at night!

That is the idyll still fondly cherished by the city-born. The reality of cottage life as the countryman knows it is, of course, a very different thing. Cottages do not always command sea views; hills do not always shelter them from the wind; they are not even always provided with a porch. John Collins would have been obliged, in his " downhill of life," to scythe his field, milk his cow, groom his horse, draw water from the well, trim hedges, prune fruit trees and, when winter came, gather fuel for his fire and clear snow from the garden path.

These activities, keeping him hard at work from dawn to dusk, would have left him with little time for the entertainment of his friends, for lotus eating or poetizing.

A Lemsford cottage

Hertfordshire, despite the population influx of the past twenty years and much incidental destruction of old buildings, has many cottages left. Gradually disappearing, they still form a characteristic and attractive feature of the countryside. Some, of unusual historical or architectural interest, have been carefully preserved and are still inhabited. There is, for example, the cottage in Bridge Road, Welwyn Garden City, close to the town centre. A building of medium size, part of it at least dates back to the sixteenth century. Though it cannot claim an exciting history it does provide a pleasant contrast with its twentieth-century surroundings.

Only a few miles away, in Lemsford village, is a cottage that may well rank as one of the most interesting in the county. The site is a pleasant one on the banks of the Lea, well sheltered from the north wind by the trees of Brocket Park—to which, indeed, it belongs. This Lemsford cottage is remarkable for both its picturesque quality and its age—the date 1734 appears conspicuously on the gable.

Its present occupants, both over eighty years of age, are remarkable too—for their long memories and intimate knowledge of the district. George Flitney, formerly a gardener at Brocket Hall, comes from an old Cromer Hyde farming family, and he well remembers the days when corn was ground at the watermill nearby. His grandfather served Lord Palmerston—prime minister of England and a former owner of Brocket Hall—as a forester.

From Lemsford it is only a short distance by car or bicycle to Coleman's Green, which proudly guards a crumbling chimney-stack, the last remnant of a cottage in which John Bunyan, the inspired tinker who wrote *Pilgrim's Progress*, is believed to have lodged and preached.

Nell Gwynne's cottage

Some of the most typical and often best-preserved cottages are those " tied " to the big farms, to the stately homes and hereditary estates. These are, of course, cottages built for the use of agricultural workers, bailiffs, gamekepers, and employees engaged in maintenance work or the like. The tied cottage is, frankly, a hangover from the feudal era, when the labourer was bound in lifelong servitude to his master and to the soil. That the system has evils is well known, yet where relations on the farm or estate are good the arrangements often work out very satisfactorily in practice. One master, one job, one cottage may well see a worker through from early manhood to a ripe old age.

Typical " estate " cottages are to be found all over Hertfordshire, and some of them are not only externally charming but very cosy inside, with electric light, television, hot water and refrigerators! There is a cottage in the grounds of Hatfield House that might have suited John Collins had he been aware of its existence. Visitors invariably pause to look at it as they cross the Park Street viaduct. This is possibly one of the most photographed cottages in the county.

Ayot St. Lawrence's famous cottage post office has also been the subject of many a snapshot. A brick-and-timber building, it dates back to the sixteenth century. Here it was that George Bernard Shaw, greatest dramatist of the century, bought his postage stamps and set the scene of one of his plays. He counted the former postmistress, Mrs. Lyth, among his friends.

To mention all the interesting cottages in Hertfordshire is obviously impossible, as there must be hundreds. Nell Gwynne's cottage, adjoining Salisbury Hall, London Colney, is a final choice. This is without doubt one of the most visited cottages. People are attracted mainly by the moated manor house at which Charles II spent some of his leisure hours. Having inspected the Hall, which has many unique features, they cross over the garden to the cottage in which the king's mistress was installed. Those romantically minded may still, perhaps, find an aura of the pretty orange-girl's presence lingering on there.

CHAPTER NINE

FORE STREET AND THE OLD PALACE, HATFIELD

TAKING the railway station as a starting point, the most obvious approach to Hatfield House, historic home of the Salisbury family, is by way of the ornamental wrought-iron gates and the main drive. A more rewarding route, however, is that which allows us to see Fore Street, unique for its literary associations and innumerable links with times past.

Among the first of the buildings to attract the visitor's eye as he leaves the town centre, with its shops and banks, will be the diminutive Eight Bells, a haunt of Charles Dickens and introduced by him into one of his most popular novels. Prominently sited at the corner of Fore Street and Park Street, it is by tradition the "small public-house " at which Bill Sikes arrived " quite tired out " and footsore one evening. He had murdered Nancy and was a fugitive from justice.

The whole vivid scene is recorded in chapter 48 of *Oliver Twist*, where we may read that " there was a fire in the tap room, and some country labourers were drinking before it. They made room for the stranger, but he sat down in the farthest corner " with his dog, which, poor beast, was limping and lame from unaccustomed exercise. Then follows the incident where an " antic fellow, half pedlar, half mountebank," enters the bar and offers his wares, including a tablet guaranteed to remove all sorts of stains from articles of clothing—" wine stains, fruit stains, beer stains, water stains, pitch stains, mud stains, blood stains! " When the merry-andrew offers to remove a stain from Sikes's hat " the murderer, with a hideous imprecation, overthrew the table and burst from the house."

Fore Street, which has a steep gradient, was once part of the Great North Road, and the coach traffic to and from London had to pass along it. During the winter months, when ice covered the cobbles, the ascent could be a perilous adventure. Passengers were often made to dismount and walk while the coachmen with their augmented teams of ten, twelve or fourteen horses struggled to the top. The climb over, there would be a halt, and the passengers, after refreshing themselves with a hot drink at the Salisbury Arms (another inn that Dickens favoured), would resume their seats.

" Busy little street "

At the back of the hostelry known as the East Indian Chief—which, like the Salisbury Arms is, alas, no more—the famous fair of St. Etheldreda or " St. Audrey " used to be held. This fair, which dates back to 1226, was an annual event lasting a full four days. Later, in 1538, it was divided into two parts—one held in June and the other in October of each year. The October fair, which persisted well into the present century, was for the sale of toys and trinkets. Exactly when the adjective " tawdry," an abbreviation of St. Audrey, found its way into the dictionary we do not know, but there it is—a handy synonym for anything that is flashy and cheap. On the opposite side of the street stands the fine old church of St. Etheldreda, the interior of which is well worth inspecting. Robert Cecil, the first Lord Salisbury, and two of our greatest prime ministers—Lord Melbourne and the third Marquess of Salisbury—lie buried there.

Dickens, as we have noted, was well acquainted with Hatfield (among other things, he saw and reported the fire that destroyed the west wing of Hatfield House in 1835), but many other writers have trodden the pavements of Fore Street—Caroline Lamb, for example, and before her Samuel Pepys and John Evelyn, the famous diarists. Nathaniel Lee, the poet who gave us the line " When Greeks joined Greeks then was the tug of war," was the son of Richard Lee, a former rector of St. Etheldreda's church. Jane Austen, too, has passed this way—as witness her reference in *Pride and Prejudice* to the " busy little street that leads to my Lord Salisbury's house." At least one other author deserves mention—Lord David Cecil, a member of the Salisbury family, whose biography of Lord Melbourne, written in a style of great charm and distinction, has deservedly become a classic.

As a matter of fact, an afternoon can be most enjoyably spent in Fore Street, especially by the artists and photographers. With its half-submerged shops, its Georgian façades and porticoes and its " olde worlde " atmosphere, it can be most beguiling.

A royal residence

The Old Palace, at the top of the hill and reached through an ancient gateway, is one of the most famous Tudor relics in the country. Originally a quadrangular building of some size, the palace underwent many changes. Three sides were demolished by Robert Cecil to provide material for the construction of Hatfield House, which lies beyond. Despite its great age, the Old Palace, or what remains of it, has been well preserved. Restorations carried out by the fourth marquess enable one to see the great hall, with its magnificent beamed roof, in something like its original condition. The exterior is marked by a severe, even forbidding, aspect, and the red brickwork has a sombre effect in any but the brightest light. Centuries of wind and rain have done little to soften the rugged outlines.

The Old Palace was completed in 1497, during the reign of Henry VII, by Cardinal Morton—for it was at that time a Church possession. From the Bishops of Ely it passed into the hands of Henry VIII and was used by him, from 1538 onwards, as a royal residence or retreat. Sickly Edward VI spent much time there, as did Henry's two daughters—Mary and Elizabeth, the latter virtually as a prisoner.

This was after Edward's death, when Mary became queen. Suspecting her sister of complicity in Sir Thomas Wyatt's plot, she had Elizabeth put under house arrest in various places: first at Ashridge in Hertfordshire, then in the Tower of London, and eventually at Hatfield, in the palace. There she remained for several years, under a cloud—her movements watched, her freedom restricted.

Boredom was occasionally relieved through the kindly efforts of Sir Thomas Pope, in whose custody she was placed. An easy-going warden, he did everything he could to make the princess's enforced retirement not only bearable but enjoyable.

At his own expense he arranged a series of hunts, masques and balls, and entertainments of all kinds, with the object of distracting his distinguished charge. Elizabeth appreciated these courtesies and, though far from satisfied with her lot, quietly waited on events. Refusing to become involved in treasonable activities, she busied herself with books, music, needlework and the general improvement of her mind, which was receptive and acute.

Memorable pageantry

On November 17, 1558, Mary died, and the news was immediately sent to Elizabeth, next in the line of succession. When the messengers from Westminster arrived she was said to have been sitting in the park under an oak tree, the remnants of which, now leafless and decaying, are among the wonders that people flock to see. Close on the heels of the messengers there came to Hatfield a procession of eminent men—nobles, courtiers and officials—to pay homage to the new queen, and the Old Palace witnessed some of the most colourful scenes of its long history.

On November 19, 1558, Elizabeth held her first privy council in the " greate halle "—in which we of the twentieth century may lunch or take our afternoon tea. Having accepted her destiny, and the crown, she proceeded to London with her retinue.

It was a vivid moment, and little imagination is required to visualize the pageant winding its way through the Hertfordshire countryside—the prancing horses, the rich habits and the gay, light-hearted riders. They were on the threshold of an era to be made memorable no less by the exploits of Drake and Raleigh, of the buccaneering adventurers who brought the wealth of the New World to our shores, than by the cultural renaissance that was to give us, among other treasures, the poetry of Edmund Spenser and Shakespeare's plays.

The courtly cavalcade on its way from Hatfield to London could know nothing of all this—though there may well have been among the riders a perceptive few who could foresee the coming changes, who sensed that before them, and the young queen in their midst, there lay a brilliant, fast-moving and exciting future.

CHAPTER TEN

PRISONER IN THE PALACE

THE son of Henry VIII and Jane Seymour, Edward VI had inherited his father's crown in 1547 and with it many troubles. He was a precocious lad but easily swayed by his elderly advisers and unable personally to grapple with state affairs. These were managed by a council of regency, of which the " Protector " Somerset was head. In the spring of 1553 the consumptive sixteen-year-old king lay mortally sick, and immediately after his death the curtain rose on one of the strangest dramas in our long history.

The Wyatt plot

Next in the line of succession was Mary Tudor, the daughter of Henry VIII and Catherine of Aragon, a small, spirited woman who had once been beautiful but was prematurely aged by personal troubles and ill health. The fact that she was half Spanish and a Catholic determined the Protestant nobles on the council, many of whom had benefited from plunder of the abbeys, to ignore her claims and place a young Protestant girl, Lady Jane Grey, on the throne.

Mary, warned of the moves afoot, hurried to Framlingham castle in Suffolk, and there unfurled her standard. A few days later she re-entered London and was accepted by the Lord Mayor and the City companies as queen, and the unfortunate Lady Jane's brief reign of nine days was over. Even then, however, Mary's position was not entirely secure. In 1554 a rebellion flared up and Sir Thomas Wyatt and the men of Kent marched on London to save Jane Grey and prevent Mary's proposed Spanish alliance. Though she had many faults, the Queen was no coward, and her show of resolution at the Guildhall successfully rallied Londoners to her side. The conspiracy failed; Wyatt was captured and, in April 1554, executed on Tower Green, a few weeks after Lady Jane Grey had suffered the same fate.

Despite the crushing of the revolt Mary's position still remained precarious. London had supported her against Wyatt but disapproved of her impending marriage to Philip II of Spain and the

Morris dancers at Verulamium.

St. Albans abbey. In the foreground is a fragment of the Roman wall that once
encircled Verulamium.

The central tower of St. Albans abbey, built entirely of brick excavated from the Roman city of Verulamium.

St. Albans—the great gateway, which survived the general destruction of the monastic buildings attached to the abbey because in 1553 the town magistrates decided to use it as a jail.

King Henry VIII. Rejecting the pope's authority, he proclaimed himself head of the Church, dissolved the monasteries and confiscated their property. The last abbot of St. Albans was Richard Boreham de Stevenache, who made the act of submission on December 5, 1539.

threatened restoration of papal authority. Many an eye was already turned in admiration upon another princess, the daughter of Henry VIII and Anne Boleyn, a young woman of twenty-one—tall, graceful, golden-haired, with a ready wit and a regal presence.

Elizabeth was at Ashridge and under suspicion as an accomplice in the Wyatt plot. The queen, whose agents had been watching her closely, decided in February 1554 to send three of her privy councillors, accompanied by a strong escort, to bring her back to London for questioning.

Elizabeth found it a city of horror and desolation, with heads and quarters exposed on the gates and a score of gallows to recall the recent butcheries. There was little on her conscience, however, and, in the event, no proofs of her complicity could be produced. Yet she was consigned to the Tower, protesting at the very moment of passing through the Traitors' Gate that she was " as true a woman to the queen's majesty as any now living."

Mary was deaf to these protestations of loyalty. Her mind, indeed, was preoccupied with thoughts of dealing with Elizabeth as she had done with Jane Grey, a course urged by her Spanish advisers.

The move to Hatfield

That intention had, for reasons of expediency, to be set aside. Elizabeth could not readily be sent to the block, for she was too popular with the people. " God save the Lady Elizabeth " they were crying out in the City streets, and in the taverns thousands of illegal leaflets were being passed round.

In such circumstances the queen could neither scheme for the execution of her sister nor bar her from the succession. Even the immediate position was a delicate one. Elizabeth could not be shut up indefinitely in the Tower, while to grant her unfettered freedom seemed an impossible course, fraught with dangers. At last Mary compromised by banishing her rival to the remote countryside.

Elizabeth was sent to Woodstock, but was later allowed to visit the court at Hampton and to live there for a time in strict seclusion. Eventually, in 1555, she was moved to Hatfield, where the rambling Old Palace, acquired by Henry VIII at the Reformation, dreamed peacefully on the summit of a hill. The building, only one wing of which remains standing today, had been used by him as a place of recreation and forced retirement for troublesome offspring. Mary had herself been a prisoner there.

D

Erected by Cardinal Morton in 1497, the Old Palace had many splendid architectural features, and was not lacking in amenities— a fortunate circumstance, since Elizabeth was destined to languish there for over three years. She made the best of an unhappy situation: applied herself to theological and other studies, learnt to play two musical instruments—the lute and virginals—and generally acted the part of demure lady, improving and enjoying herself. There were walks in the park, boating parties on the Broadwater, forays into the villages. Occasionally Sir Thomas Pope, in whose charge she had been placed, arranged a hunting expedition for her. In 1556, at Shrovetide, the hospitable warden staged a " great and rich maskinge " in the hall of the palace, and on that occasion nobles and ladies of honour " apparelled in crimson satin " were in attendance on the princess.

The accession

By that time Mary, disillusioned in her marriage with Philip. was already a sick woman, and covering her name with odium because of her persecutions. The " fires of Smithfield " crackled round the body of the first martyr in February 1555, and before the end of the year six more had suffered. Latimer and Ridley were burnt at Oxford, Cranmer perished at the stake in 1556, and by October 1558 no fewer than 300 people had paid the supreme penalty for their religious convictions. The last heretic was burnt at Canterbury on November 10, and exactly a week later Mary— " bloody Mary " as she came to be called—died at St. James's, a woman embittered, detested and childless.

The news spread rapidly throughout the City, and it was still morning when, on November 17, 1558, Elizabeth learnt of her accession to the throne. She was twenty-five years old, in the full bloom of womanhood, and already distinguished by a queenly bearing and dignity. She had a ready wit, expressive eyes, a fine figure and beautiful hands. No wonder that the courtiers and statesmen who had journeyed to Hatfield with the fateful news were captivated by her, and ready to make her their idol.

On the following day, in the great hall of the Old Palace, Elizabeth held her first privy council, and appointed Sir William Cecil, Lord Burghley, to be her secretary of state—a propitious move, as it proved, for he was a man of genius and ability. Another day or two passed and then the queen left Hatfield to show herself to her expectant subjects in the capital.

Accompanied by 1,000 lords and ladies she arrived at the Charterhouse, and was presently on her way to the Tower, no longer a prisoner but a sovereign—" clad in purple velvet and a scarf about her neck." Citizens welcomed her with speeches, singing, dancing, and " playing with regals," and such shooting of guns as had never been heard before.

Long reign

After five years of darkness and horror, England's golden age of art, literature and exploration was about to begin. The music of Morley, Byrd and Tallis; the poetry of Edmund Spenser and Shakespeare; the defeat of the Armada—all belong to this astonishing period. Before Elizabeth's long reign was over Sir Walter Raleigh had founded the first American settlement of Virginia, London's merchant-adventurers were sending their fleets to the coasts of Africa and the East Indies, and Drake had circumnavigated the globe.

Taking all these achievements into account, it may be said without exaggeration that November 17, 1558, was a day of supreme importance not only for Hertfordshire but for all English-speaking peoples.

CHAPTER ELEVEN

HATFIELD HOUSE AND ITS ART TREASURES

THE home of the Cecil family during Queen Elizabeth's reign had been at Theobalds, near Cheshunt, in east Hertfordshire, and there it might have remained to the present day had not James I taken a liking to the house and its surroundings. The area abounded with wild deer and other game, and the king, like so many other monarchs from Rufus onwards, was devoted to the pleasures of the chase. James therefore suggested to Robert Cecil, then Lord Treasurer, that he should give up Theobalds and take Hatfield with its Old Palace in exchange. Cecil, though his reactions were unfavourable, chose to regard the proposal as a command, and accepted. The king, however, undertook to help him build an entirely new house.

As a result of this agreement work commenced in 1607, and within five years Hatfield House was completed, a magnificent edifice of brick and Caen stone. Unfortunately, Robert Cecil did not live long enough to make it his residence, for he was a very sick man in 1612, and died while on his way to Hatfield from Bath, where he had gone to take the waters. At the top of Fore Street, close to the house, is the old church of St. Etheldreda, and there beneath a white marble monument he lies buried.

Physically Robert Cecil was unremarkable—he lacked stature and was hump-backed, a misfortune that the contemporary style of clothing tended to exaggerate. A sensitive man, he was extremely conscious of the deformity, and suffered when political opponents made sly references to it, which they did often enough. The queen dubbed him affectionately her " pygmy," but her successor, James, was blunter and could apply such epithets as " monkey," " parrot-monger " and " fool." Cecil, however, had a cool head and a strong character, and put up a calm front to such railings.

Having served Elizabeth with great zeal as Secretary of State, Cecil was retained by James when he ascended the throne. Not only was the little man with the crooked shoulders made responsible for managing the country's finances, the most complicated part of which concerned the king's debts, but he was given a voice in the formation of national policy, and England was at that time not without her enemies abroad.

Cecil, therefore, bore a heavy burden, but displayed conspicuous ability in discharging his duties and maintaining the dignity of his office. He successfully countered many of the Machiavellian intrigues of the court, and managed to hold his own against the gentlemen of fortune who surrounded the person of the king.

Tapestries, paintings

Of the architectural splendours of Hatfield House little need be said, though the great Jacobean mansion is, of course, one of the finest examples of its kind in the country. Everyone admires the imposing south front and the Renaissance features it incorporates, of which the clock tower and the arches underneath may in particular be noted. These arches, as is clearly shown in a number of old prints, were at one time open to the central court, and were only filled in at a later date.

There is doubt as to the name of the architect, who may have been one John Thorpe, but it is more probable that Cecil, aided by a competent clerk of the works, a good mason and a carpenter, made his own plans. The building, which cost £10,000, is in the form of the letter E—two wings being joined together by a connecting block of some considerable length.

A volume might quite easily be written about the actual construction of Hatfield House, drawing on the detailed records that Cecil kept, and another one about the art treasures—the tapestries, paintings, woodcarvings, old furniture and silver with which it has since been filled. Here it is possible to mention only some of the more outstanding items of interest.

Visitors to the house are normally admitted by way of the door in the Jacobean north front. From the entrance lobby there is immediate access to the fine banqueting hall, which, with its oriel window, its minstrels' gallery and carved screen, is in the medieval rather than the Elizabethan tradition. The painted roof, the mural frescoes, the Brussels tapestries and faded Napoleonic flags, presented by Wellington after Waterloo, all combine to give the apartment an air of historic dignity.

King James's drawing room, the principal state apartment, is notable for the plaster statue of the king that occupies a place over the mantelpiece, as well as for its eighteenth-century furniture and family portraits. The grand staircase, with its carved wood pillars and gates (provided to keep dogs on the ground floor), is also a feature of major interest.

The famous long gallery, running across the south front, is stated to be the longest in the country. Measuring nearly 200 feet from end to end, it is chiefly remarkable for its gilded roof, its furnishings and its curiosities—among which are included the garden hat and silk stockings worn by Elizabeth during her stay at the Old Palace, where her sister Mary kept her a prisoner.

Immediately beneath the long gallery is the armoury, in which are many fine specimens of sixteenth-century armour, perfectly maintained and always in bright, shining condition. Four large tapestries hanging on the walls, representing the seasons, were woven in Gloucestershire in the early seventeenth century, and are among the most faultless of their kind in existence. A little faded in colour, they are nevertheless well preserved and give us charming glimpses of country life 300 years ago. They have, therefore, a documentary as well as an artistic value.

Famous portraits

Two other parts of Hatfield House not to be missed are the winter drawing room, with its portraits of James I, Charles I and George III, and the tiny chapel situated in the west wing of the building. The stained-glass windows will immediately attract the eye because of their gorgeous colouring and great beauty. The glass, which is of Flemish origin, was put in place by Robert Cecil himself in the seventeenth century.

Hatfield House library comprises a fine collection of old books, many of them illuminated and of considerable value. The family archives, as may well be imagined, are stacked full of state documents and correspondence covering the reigns of Elizabeth and James, when the Cecils were playing leading roles in the affairs of the country. Lord Burghley's personal diary, in which the defeat of the Spanish Armada is recorded, is another of the priceless literary treasures.

Before leaving Hatfield House for a glimpse of the lovely gardens, visitors should make a point of inspecting three unique portraits. All are of Queen Elizabeth and the work of painters—among them the court miniaturist—who knew her personally. The one depicting her as " The Mistress Diana," by Cornelius Vroom, is perhaps the least interesting. Nicholas Hilliard's " ermine " portrait, on the other hand, is a work of some excellence. The queen is shown wearing a dress with ermine-fur ornamentation on the sleeves and a mass of jewellery, the overall effect of which is most arresting. Apart from its decorative qualities the painting was probably also a good likeness.

The most famous portrait of Elizabeth to be seen at Hatfield is, however, the " rainbow " portrait. Hanging at the foot of the grand staircase already mentioned, the picture focuses attention because of its unusual character and beautiful design. Though the style is formal and outmoded, Elizabeth's cool self-possession, imperiousness and dignity—in which there is an element of maidenly primness—are well conveyed. Her costume will be seen, on close examination, to be patterned with human ears and eyes, which symbolized her ability to hear all and to see all. The great serpent on her sleeve is, of course, one of the most ancient insignia of royalty.

In her hand Elizabeth holds a rainbow, and there is a motto just above it which reads *Non sine sole iris* (" No rainbow without the sun "). In its own way the picture is a masterpiece, immortalizing both the virgin queen and the painter, Zuccaro, whose observant eye, imagination and skill brought it into being.

CHAPTER TWELVE

AMELIA, THE HARUM-SCARUM

APART from its record of royal visitors the annals of Hatfield House are comparatively uneventful. Fortune did not call upon it to play the part of a beleaguered fortress, nor was it ever sacked and pillaged. Once, however, it came near to being destroyed by fire.

The story of that near-disaster began when James, the seventh Earl of Salisbury, married the high-spirited Lady Mary Amelia Hill, whose portrait by Sir Joshua Reynolds shows her as a tall, stately person dressed in a flowing silk gown, her powdered hair piled high on her head in eighteenth-century style.

Having seen her husband created first marquess and appointed Lord Chamberlain to George III, she set about re-equipping Hatfield House, which had become dilapidated, with fine new furniture, silverware and rare china. So wholeheartedly did she throw herself into this task that the great mansion was quickly restored to something like its former glory. Amelia, though wildly extravagant, had good taste.

There was, however, a rebellious streak in her nature, and she succeeded as a result of unconventional behaviour—such as playing cards on Sunday—in scandalizing many of her more respectable friends. Amelia had certainly a passion for card-playing, and it is on record that she was once found in the long gallery early in the morning, after a reckless gambling bout, ankle deep in cards! The custom, it should be explained, was to use a new pack of cards after every game to avoid shuffling.

She liked parties, throwing money away, and being rowed about on the Broadwater in a state barge.

The gutted west wing

Lady Amelia was also a keen sportswoman, with a particular interest in fox-hunting. Indeed, it is legendary that she rode to hounds on the very last day of her life, when eighty-five years of age. Because of her infirmities and failing eyesight she had on that occasion to be strapped to her horse. Nevertheless, with patrician pluck, she insisted on jumping over every hedge, ditch and fence with the rest of the field. The story goes that she had a groom at her side, an old and trusted servant one imagines, because of the forthright speech he permitted himself to use.

Whenever they approached an obstacle the groom would shout " Jump, my lady, jump," and if she did not respond at once the cry would be repeated louder: " Jump, my lady, *damn you*, jump! " They must have made a remarkable pair as they careered madly over the wet fields in pursuit of the uneatable!

Hatfield House, under the imperious rule of Marchioness Amelia, became a well-known Tory stronghold. She was given the nickname " Old Sarum " by the Whig radicals, and the wits made up lampoons about her in which " Sarum " was made to rhyme, not very originally, with " harum-scarum." A woman of quality and character, she could, however, afford to snap her fingers at the writers of such trite doggerel.

Now for the story of the fire. The marchioness (or rather dowager marchioness as she then was) retired to her room in the west wing of Hatfield House late one night. Old, eccentric, almost blind, and tired with her exertions in the hunt, she began testily searching for notepaper and pen. A maid was the last to see her alive—laboriously writing a letter by the light of two flickering candles.

Peace enveloped the household; then, half an hour later, another servant, undertaking some last-minute errand, saw a dense cloud of smoke emerging from Amelia's room into the well of the staircase. The fire spread rapidly, and soon many of the adjoining apartments were ablaze. The roof crashed in, and when at last the rescuers could enter the old lady's room it was too late. She was found dead among the smoking debris. One of the candles, it was concluded by the searchers, had toppled over, setting light to Amelia's writing table.

The west wing of Hatfield House was gutted, and but for a lucky chance the entire building might have been destroyed. Fortunately, at a critical moment the wind changed and, because of the excessive heat, a tank burst in the roof. A spurt of molten lead was followed by a cascade of water, and so the greater part of the stately home was spared.

Dickens reports

The fire as seen from picturesque Fore Street, Hatfield, is vividly described in the following eye-witness account: " Rising into the air with showers of sparks and rolling one above the other were sheets of flame lighting the atmosphere for miles around. There were half-dressed figures tearing to and fro, some endeavouring to drag frightened horses from the stables, others coming laden from the burning pile, amidst a shower of burning sparks and the tumbling down of red-hot beams. The apertures, where doors and windows stood half an hour earlier, disclosed a mass of raging fire.''

The passage is quoted from *Oliver Twist*, the novel by Charles Dickens, who in 1835—when these events occurred—was a busy young newspaper reporter.

CHAPTER THIRTEEN

THE THIRD MARQUESS OF SALISBURY—LAST OF THE EMINENT VICTORIANS

THE Cecil family, whose home at Hatfield is one of the stateliest in England, first attained to high eminence in the Elizabethan period. William Cecil Burghley was the shrewd, competent minister on whom the queen depended for management of her affairs during the early and middle years of her reign. Towards the end, when Burghley died, she placed an almost equal confidence in his son Robert Cecil, whom she appointed Secretary of State, a position of responsibility and honour. When Elizabeth died, Robert Cecil became chief minister to James I, who created him Earl of Salisbury in 1605 and gave him—in exchange for Theobalds—the estate on which Hatfield House now stands.

After that period of brilliance, however, the Cecil family declined in importance, and produced no outstanding figure for over 200 years. The record is, indeed, one of extravagance, mediocrity, irresponsibility, aristocratic pride, and preoccupation with the fluctuating family fortunes. Only in early Victorian times, under the second marquess, did the long period of decline show signs of drawing to an end. With the third marquess the family image was fully restored, and the Cecils won back the reputation that their Elizabethan and Jacobean ancestors had enjoyed.

Inheriting the title

Robert Arthur Gascoyne Talbot Cecil, destined to be three times prime minister and four times foreign secretary of Great Britain, was born in 1830. His education at Eton and Christ Church, Oxford, was of the kind usual for a young man of his class. Returned to the House of Commons in 1853, he quickly made a name for himself as a pungent and persuasive, if not actually an eloquent, speaker. The two main political parties at that time were the Conservatives and the Liberals, and it was, of course, as a representative of the Conservative cause that Cecil had been elected.

In 1857 he married Georgina Alderson, a step that did not meet with his father's approval. As a result the couple appear to have been in straitened circumstances for some time, and it was with a view to augmenting his income that Robert Cecil began writing for the press. His essays in the *Saturday Review*, as vigorous and incisive as the speeches he made, attracted much attention. Robert had an elder brother who would in the normal course of events have succeeded to the title. In 1865 this brother died, whereupon Robert acquired the courtesy title of Viscount Cranbourne, and became the legal heir. When his father, James, the second marquess, died in 1868 Robert was translated from the Commons to the House of Lords, and became master of the Hatfield estate.

By that time he had already made his mark as a politician of ability. In 1866 he had been appointed Secretary of State for India, and it was apparent to many that his progress through the corridors of power would be swift and sure.

The statesman

Living as we do in a democratic age, it is difficult to realize that so many things we now take for granted were still, in Victorian times, controversial issues capable of arousing the fiercest passions. For example, universal suffrage and the secret ballot were matters ardently advocated by one side and doggedly resisted by the other. Compulsory elementary education was not achieved until 1870, and the welfare state—with provisions for the sick, the unemployed and the aged—was to the Victorian mind an altogether alien concept.

Unlike his compeer Disraeli, the third marquess had a deep distrust of democracy and of the common man, and thought that any extension of the franchise would imperil the rights of property owners and of those whose privilege it had always been to rule. Democracy he regarded as a threat to freedom, and education of the masses as a not altogether desirable necessity. In the domestic sphere, therefore, his political credo was one of maintaining things as they were and resisting change.

Salisbury's foreign policy was based, according to his own words, on the simple principles of " upholding England's honour steadily and fearlessly," and non-interference in the affairs of other nations. These excellent precepts, however, seem to have coexisted with the view that coloured people, such as the " Hottentots and Hindus," were incapable of self government and that it was quite natural that their affairs should be managed for them by their white superiors. Such ideas were not peculiar to him, but formed part of the contemporary way of thought.

That Lord Salisbury was respected, and that he made a profound impact on his times, not even his more captious modern critics would deny. Indeed, it is generally conceded that he had a talent for foreign affairs and was also one of the greatest prime ministers this country has ever had. His three periods of office as leader of the country total nearly fourteen years, and in this respect at least he scored a triumph over Gladstone, his implacable Liberal opponent, whose tenure of the premiership was just under thirteen years.

Life at Hatfield

In his private, as in his political, life the third marquess was distinguished by the benevolent paternalism that in Victorian times was held up as the ideal to be followed by all who were wealthy or exercised authority. Something of an enigma to the world at large, he appears to have been understood and well liked by a small inner circle of friends and acquaintances. He was, of course, a man of culture, of principle and integrity—even, perhaps, of vision. People were ready to give him their confidence, and the image that he has left behind him, of a dignified and respected father figure, was by no means undeserved.

When at Hatfield, Lord Salisbury's day invariably began with prayers in the chapel which forms part of the west wing of the noble Jacobean house. He was, in the true Victorian fashion, a deeply religious man and a student—as his library testifies—of theology. At the same time he took a keen interest in scientific matters, and not only read all the literature on the subject but maintained an experimental laboratory. His earliest interest had been in chemistry, but later he turned to the study of electricity, and in 1881 arranged for electric light to be installed in Hatfield House, which was, in fact, the first country house to be so equipped. Some years after that he ordered the house to be wired for internal telephones, and had some of the windows fitted with plate glass— which was then a new invention. Little interested in sport, he nevertheless liked riding about in Hatfield Park—on a tricycle.

Despite these gestures, and an obviously genuine desire to be modern and progressive, it is probably true that science alarmed him a little—if only because it undermined so many of his most dearly held philosophical and theological beliefs. He found it hard, for example, to accept Darwin's theory of evolution.

Distinguished visitors

Under James, the second marquess, Hatfield House had been restored to something like its former glory. He had completely rebuilt the west wing, destroyed by fire in 1835, and had carried out many alterations. By the time that Lord Salisbury entered into his patrimony in 1868 the ancestral home was again fit for the reception of royal and other distinguished visitors. He himself took great pride in the house, in the art treasures it contained, and in the gardens which his father had laid out.

From the time that the third marquess became foreign secretary and a figure on the world stage, in 1878, he was called upon to entertain many important guests. Hatfield House, in fact, became a rendezvous where foreign heads of state—such as the emperor of Germany and the king of Italy—forgathered to discuss international affairs. Hospitality was extended to ambassadors, to Ministers of the Crown, Members of Parliament, and other men who had a voice in the affairs of the nation. On at least two occasions Queen Victoria was welcomed at Hatfield House: once in 1846 when, accompanied by Prince Albert, she attended a state ball, and again in 1887, during Lord Salisbury's second period of office as prime minister. This was considered such an historic event that the Great Northern Railway built a special waiting room on Hatfield station for the queen's reception. It was, of course, the year of her jubilee.

Entertainments of a homelier kind took place every Christmas Eve, when the master of Hatfield House threw a party for the benefit of local people—more particularly his tenants and cottagers.

The last years

Lord Salisbury's political burdens were often of an onerous nature, particularly towards the end of his life. Four times between 1895 and 1900 Britain found herself on the brink of major wars but was able to overcome the crises. The Boer War, which broke out in 1899, he was unable to avert, but he resolutely saw it through, refusing to retire until it was ended. Peace in South Africa was restored in May 1902, and a few months later the grand old man of Hatfield, champion of the old order against the new, considered his duty done and retired. He died in August of the following year, aged seventy-three, and was buried by the side of his wife in the small burial ground adjacent to Hatfield church.

CHAPTER FOURTEEN

LEMSFORD—THE VILLAGE WITH A SONG IN ITS HEART

ONCE described by Elizabeth I as " the prettiest village in England," Lemsford is now no more than a straggle of cottages and inns on either side of a narrow, winding road —an unashamed piece of ribbon development without architectural or other pretensions. Lemsford is homely, unromantic, and only just beginning to be affected by the prevailing winds of change.

At its eastern end, close to the A1 road, are a number of allotments on which the villagers grow their vegetables, an extensive watercress bed, and a motoring roundabout carved out of an old chalk quarry. Northwards are rolling hillsides with clumps of apple trees and hedgerows of bramble and dog-rose. Meandering through lush meadows to the south one finds the River Lea, Isaak Walton's Lea—still, despite many discouragements, inhabited by a variety of fish.

Vanished inn sign

Crossing a tiny bridge, which marks the site of a previous ford, the village centre is reached. Here are a number of cottages (one bearing the date 1734 on its gable), an old Georgian house and a grocery store. This, the Old Mill Store, was formerly a smithy, and there are still elderly people in Lemsford who remember watching the smith—Herbert Young—hammering away at his anvil and making the sparks fly. Two inns provide rallying centres for inhabitants and visitors.

One of these inns, the Long Arm and Short Arm, has excited the interest of antiquarians and journalists for decades. " What is the origin of the curious name?" they ask.

There is a stock answer for this. Once upon a time there hung outside the inn a picturesque sign depicting a horse-drawn wagon and two men—the wagoner extending his arm at full length for a tankard of beer which the landlord was holding but with his arm held back. To make the meaning absolutely clear the sign incorcorporated a motto: " Pay before you sip." A well-known artist, George Frederick Herring, is said to have painted the sign on his way to the Doncaster races, and the legend is that because of its

The church of St. Peter, where after the second battle of St. Albans Yorkist troops were buried in a mass grave.

A cottage in the country with all modern conveniences. Taken at Lemsford, near Welwyn Garden City.

The population expansion has placed a premium on Hertfordshire cottages. They are eagerly bought up, reconstructed, and equipped with modern labour-saving devices. This attractive house at Digswell, near Welwyn, once consisted of no fewer than four tiny cottages.

An Arcadian gem in the heart of old Hatfield. Seen and admired by thousands of visitors on their way to Hatfield House, this cottage has a delightful setting on a hillside overlooking a road along which the horse coaches once ran.

Georgian houses in Fore Street, Hatfield.

Fore Street, Hatfield. The distant view through the lodge gate is admired by all who see it, but the window with its diamond panes and the fine wistaria plant framing the arch also claim attention.

The Old Palace, Hatfield, where Princess Elizabeth was kept under house arrest.

Hatfield House, a magnificent edifice of brick and Caen stone, was completed in 1612.

Reproduced by courtesy of the Marquess of Salisbury, K.G., P.C.

The famous " rainbow portrait " of Elizabeth I, which hangs in
Hatfield House.

Reproduced by courtesy of the National Portrait Gallery.

William Cecil, Lord Burghley (1520-98), the father of Robert Cecil. Painting attributed to Marcus Gheeraerts the Younger.

The armoury at Hatfield House. The suits of armour were worn by Spaniards at the time of the Armada and date from the sixteenth century. The arches on the right were once open, but were filled in with glass, about 1830, by the second Marquess of Salisbury, who also laid the black and white marble floor.

high artistic value it was either acquired by a wealthy collector or stolen.

Though research has tended to confirm the story, it seems probable that there is a simpler explanation for the name Long Arm and Short Arm, namely that in times past, particularly when winter flood-water made the ford dangerous, the landlord of the inn would put out two wooden arms, one long and one short, to indicate a safe or unsafe passage. Such signs are still in use at ford crossings.

The Brocket cup

Just at the back of the inn, poised on the hillside, is a cottage which for a time was the home of a colourful Regency character. Tom Barclay was an athlete, six feet tall, strong as an ox, who brought pugilists to Lemsford for training purposes. A great fighter himself, he had perfected methods then considered unorthodox. He took his prizefighters for long walks in Brocket Park, put them on a carefully regulated diet, and made them go early to bed! Tom Cribb, the English champion, a friend of Lord Byron, was perhaps the most famous of Tom Barclay's bare-knuckle fighters to be trained in Lemsford village.

Close to the bridge, on the other side of the Lea, is a stile marking the beginning of a footpath across Brocket—one of the most historic parks in the county. The beeches, cypresses and cedars were planted by Capability Brown, the celebrated landscape gardener. Inside the park, to the right, will be seen an upward-rising slope known as The Valley, which in its day has been a racecourse. One of the most frequent visitors to Lemsford races was the Prince Regent, afterwards King George IV, " the first gentleman of Europe " and an enthusiastic patron of the turf. The course, a rival to Ascot, was laid out early in the nineteenth century, and the race for the Brocket cup came to be regarded as one of the leading events in the sporting calendar.

Christmas favourite

Lemsford mill, formerly the property of a well-known Hatfield miller, is now used for quite different purposes. Older residents can, however, still remember the days when processions of horse-drawn wagons brought loads of corn to the mill to be ground into flour. They also treasure memories of the popular song which the mill and its surroundings are said to have inspired, and which their parents

E

sang seventy or eighty years ago. The words have a sentimental
ring:

> *" There's an old mill by the stream,*
> *Nelly Dean,*
> *Where we used to sit and dream,*
> *Nelly Dean;*
> *And the waters as they flow*
> *Seem to murmur soft and low,*
> *" You're my heart's desire,*
> *I love you,*
> *Nelly Dean. "*

A great favourite at Christmas time, it was written by J. P. Skelly,
a musician who in Victorian times was a celebrity. The story goes
that he was a guest at Brocket Hall, and came one day to have a
look at the Lemsford scene. The village enchanted him as it has
countless others. When a pretty girl appeared on the wooden bridge
that then spanned the river the susceptible composer's heart was
fired, and so he wrote his song, using homely Hertfordshire words
that in time came to be known the world over.

CHAPTER FIFTEEN

THE ROMANCE OF WILLIAM AND CAROLINE LAMB

NO blue blood flowed in the veins of the Lambs, and they had no proud or aristocratic forebears. Their emergence from obscurity was largely due to the money-making ability of Peniston Lamb, an astute Nottingham attorney. When he died in 1734 he had amassed a fortune of £100,000, which he left to his nephew Matthew Lamb, who made such good use of his inheritance that eventually it was increased tenfold. Matthew in 1746 purchased Brocket Hall in central Hertfordshire and the 500 acres of land on which it stood. In 1755 he was created a baronet.

Sir Matthew and his wife had three children, including a son, Peniston, who when his father died in 1768 succeeded to the family fortune and the title. Peniston appears to have been a very ordinary person, semi-literate and possessing only one obvious talent—for squandering the money that his predecessors had acquired by their hard work and professional skill. Wealth, however, is a universal passport and opened many doors to him that would otherwise have remained shut. In 1781 he became first Viscount Melbourne, and was found a place in Parliament, which he attended for over forty years without once making a speech!

For all his mediocrity Melbourne had been remarkably fortunate in his marriage, for his wife, *née* Elizabeth Milbanke, was a woman of intelligence and character, who charmed everyone with whom she came into contact. Lady Melbourne was not only beautiful but of a practical nature, and could do anything from managing the estate at Brocket to planning a friend's or relative's political career. She was also ambitious, and constituted the driving force that gradually raised the family to a position of power and prestige.

The Hertfordshire home

The Melbournes were well pleased with Brocket Hall, the elegant brick mansion that had been completely rebuilt by the famous architect James Paine, under the direction of Sir Matthew Lamb soon after he had acquired it. Normally it was at Brocket that the Melbournes lived, though they also had a fine town house. At

Brocket, in healthy and peaceful country surroundings, they brought up their six children. Peniston, the eldest son, disappointed his father by dying at a comparatively early age. William Lamb, born in 1779 and his mother's favourite, then became heir to the estate and to the title. There was a third son, Frederick (better known as Lord Beauvale), who later carved out a successful career for himself in the diplomatic service. One of the two daughters died young, but the other, Emily (1787-1869), married twice—first Earl Cowper and then, after a brief widowhood, Lord Palmerston—and lived to a ripe old age.

The head of the family, as we have seen, was a somewhat stupid, feckless character, fond of hunting and drinking, who left all major decisions to his wife and accepted her dominance, as well as her infidelities, with resigned patience. Life at Brocket was nevertheless pleasant enough. Lady Melbourne, with her admiring friends and children, who all adored her, rode gaily about the park on horseback. Periodically there were parties and banquets, when the rooms of the stately mansion were full of high-spirited conversation and laughter.

It was on one of these festive occasions that William Lamb, a serious young man of twenty-one, first became acquainted with Lady Bessborough's daughter Caroline, an impetuous, imaginative and excitable child of fourteen, whose personality and elfin beauty impressed him deeply. He, with his equable temperament and manly good looks, had a like effect on her. Marriage, of course, did not enter the thoughts of either at that time, but the attraction was already there, tacitly admitted and destined to grow stronger.

Eton and Cambridge

The early education of William Lamb, the future Lord Melbourne and prime minister, began simply enough in a Hertfordshire village school. Though a clever boy, he did not work very hard at his lessons, preferring to stare out of the windows and watch what was going on in the fields. Later, when nine years of age, he left Brocket for Eton, with ten guineas in his pocket and the blessing of his brilliant mother, who had already decided that he was the most talented of her six children and with a little pushing on her part would go far. At Eton William appears to have adjusted himself to the public-school routine—with its floggings, fisticuffs and other severities—easily enough. Eight years later he went to Cambridge, where, as at Brocket and Eton, he displayed a greater liking for the pursuit of pleasure than for learning. Nevertheless, he read widely and developed a taste for the classics of literature that was to last and sustain him to the end of his life. At Cambridge, too, he began to display a more positive interest in politics and public affairs, and distinguished himself by winning the prize in a competition for oratory. This brought him to the notice of Charles James Fox, the Whig statesman, who was himself an eloquent speaker and debater. It was just after leaving Cambridge that, on a visit to Brocket, he met Caroline Ponsonby, the girl with the golden hair and irrepressible flow of conversation, as already related.

However, William's mother did not consider her son's education was yet finished. She arranged for him and his brother Frederick to be sent to Glasgow University, where, for the first time, he was forced into unrelenting study. Later, when he had returned to Brocket, the question of a career had to be faced. After some hesitation he decided to become a lawyer, and in 1804 was called to the Bar. There is no record, however, of his ever having had a brief.

In the following year his elder brother, Peniston, died, and he became the legal heir.

Marriage

Caroline Ponsonby had by then developed into a sophisticated young woman of nineteen, and the more William saw of her the more he was dazzled by her ethereal charm, intelligence, wit, beauty and physical vitality. Yet she was a frail, slight person, known to her friends as " Ariel " or the " Fairy Queen," and in appearance still very much the child he had met at the Brocket Hall party. He knew, of course, that there was another side to her character, that she liked having her own way and when thwarted would lose her temper and abuse those about her with uncontrollable fury. Everyone knew of her neurotic tendencies, but it made no difference to William, who soon after the improvement in his prospects wrote to Caroline declaring that he had loved her " deeply, dearly and faithfully " for several years. A few days later—with the approval of Lady Bessborough, her mother—she accepted his proposal and they became engaged.

There is no doubt about their happiness in the days that followed, despite some differences of opinion between the prospective mothersin-law, and the preparations for the wedding went ahead with little to mar the serenity of the young couple. Only as the day of the ceremony approached did Caroline, her nerves at breaking point, reveal the tempestuous, hysterical side of her nature. At the close of the wedding service she found fault with the officiating bishop, tore her gown in anger, and had to be carried away in a dead faint.

William, full of solicitude, bore off his bride to the gracious Hertfordshire park in which their honeymoon was to be spent. It was midsummer, with the water foaming white under the arches of the Palladian bridge and the cuckoo calling from among the lush foliage of the trees. At Brocket Caroline recovered; the brilliant June sunshine dissipated her mood of melancholy and she was herself again—bewitching, tender, gay, galloping round the park like a tomboy, painting watercolours, and listening while William read aloud from his favourite poets.

Entry into politics

He was then twenty-six, and in the following year, under pressure from Lady Melbourne and his friends, decided to take up a career in politics. In January 1806 he made his entry into the House of Commons as the member for Leominster, and eventually, after various vicissitudes, was elected M.P. for the Hertford constituency. All through this period, however, he displayed little of political conviction or zeal. His attendances at the House were irregular, and critics declared that there was a " streak of idleness " in William Lamb's nature and that he would never rise to any high position.

However, the Whig aristocracy thought highly of him, admitted him into their conclaves and marked him as at least a possible leader. When his father died in 1828 William became the second viscount and shortly afterwards was offered, and accepted, the home secretaryship. He became prime minister for the first time in 1834, at the age of fifty-five.

CHAPTER SIXTEEN

A BONFIRE OF BYRON'S LETTERS

THE marriage of William Lamb and Caroline Ponsonby in the summer of 1805 was one of those disastrous unions doomed from the very first to unhappiness and failure. Caroline's nerve-storm after the London wedding ceremony proved to be the prelude to other uncontrollable, and even wilder, outbursts. William, who was kindly and indulgent to a degree, was loath to believe that his young wife might actually be insane, yet that suspicion had been present in the minds of her own family even when she was a child.

Born in 1785, Caroline was the only daughter of the third Earl of Bessborough, and had been sent at three years of age to Italy, with only a servant to look after her. On her return to England six years later she had joined her mother, also a most captivating woman, in the Bessboroughs' Cavendish Square household. Caroline had become one of the " Devonshire House girls " and there, among her cousins, she was educated in the style befitting her station as a nobleman's daughter. She absorbed all that was most refined in the culture of the period—its art, its music, its poetry. She moved continuously in an atmosphere of intellectual enlightenment and emotional tranquillity. All this should have had a stabilizing effect on her excitable nature, yet she developed in such an abnormal way that her grandmother, Lady Spencer, into whose care she passed, became worried and consulted a doctor to establish whether she was or was not mentally deranged.

The doctor's pronouncement is unknown, but it was probably of a non-committal and reassuring nature. Caroline grew up and married William Lamb, who before he became Viscount Melbourne had not been considered a suitable match for her, and whom she had therefore refused.

Infatuation

There had been a scene at the wedding, but for a time at least, while at Brocket, their married life was happy. Then, all too quickly, came the first rifts in the lute, the first misunderstandings, and the first quarrels. In 1807 their son, Augustus Lamb, was born—with little effect on their worsening relationship. Five years later, when Caroline met Lord Byron for the first time, it looked as if the ill-assorted marriage would break up in mutual disenchantment and anger.

Byron, whose first two cantos of *Childe Harold* profoundly impressed literary London in 1812, swept Caroline completely off her feet. She managed to strike up an acquaintance with him, and presently tried to snatch him away from his other admirers and make him her own exclusive property. Knowing full well, as her diary testifies, that he was " mad, bad and dangerous," she yet allowed herself to become wildly infatuated—though it was probably more with his reputation than with his person. Byron, though handsome, had a club foot and was far from being the assured, polished man of the world that he pretended to be.

When it came to Caroline's ears that the poet had declared their friendship to be at an end, and that he was flirting with other women, the floodgates of hysteria were again opened. Caroline fled with her broken heart to Brocket Hall, and kept William awake all night with her alternate lamentations and screams of jealous rage. When news came that Byron had proposed marriage to Lady Melbourne's niece, Annabella Milbanke, and when, further, he wrote to Caroline telling her bluntly to put a check on her vanity and to exert her caprices on others, the shock was so severe that the unfortunate lady completely lost control of herself.

The affair with Byron came to an end in 1813, and William Lamb, seeing his wife so tormented and irrational, came to the conclusion that their marriage was an utter failure and that he must seek a separation.

The bonfire

It was while the legal formalities were in progress that Caroline wrote her first novel, *Glenarvon*, described as a " rhapsodical tale," in which she caricatured Byron as the heartless, fickle lover. The writing was done clandestinely and in strange circumstances: Caroline worked by candlelight in Brocket Hall at dead of night, and kept her labours a secret from everyone except a governess.

When Byron read *Glenarvon* he remarked that it would have been more entertaining if it had been more truthful. Later he condemned it roundly as a completely " insincere production," and scornfully dismissed the caricature of himself with the comment that the portrait was bound to be poor as he had " not sat for it very long "! Someone at once passed on his remarks to Lady Caroline, with the result that her romantic illusions about the poet were again rudely shattered. She lit a bonfire in Brocket Park and burned his letters and the miniature portrait he had given to her.

Several girls from the village were brought in to witness the holocaust. Dressed in white garments, they were made to whirl round the flames in a fantastic dance, and to recite verses that Caroline had especially composed for the occasion. What the Lemsford damsels thought of the bizarre rigmarole in which they were participating can only be guessed. The ritual of the bonfire, as far as Caroline was concerned, seems to have had a cathartic effect, but the period of emotional calm that followed proved to be very short-lived, for soon afterwards she was bombarding Byron with letters that were a fine mixture of flattery and abuse. They met again twice—the first time in private, the second time at a glittering social function.

Lady Heathcote's ball provided the occasion for the climax of their troubled relationship. Caroline had gone with the intention of making one final bid for Byron's affection and loyalty. Her gaiety and her choice of gallant waltzing partners were meant to arouse his jealousy, but he saw through the manœuvre and when they exchanged a few words during the course of the evening was politely sarcastic. Caroline—piqued and very much upset—then staged the most dramatic scene of her life. Rushing into the drawing room, she broke a glass and gashed her arms with the jagged splinters! Only the prompt intervention of Lady Melbourne saved her from serious injury or even death.

The incident created a sensation when reported in the London newspapers next day. Dazed and defeated and shamed, for her conduct had put her outside the pale of fashionable society, Caroline crept back to the quiet of the Hertfordshire countryside.

Reconciliation

There was no one to whom she could turn for sympathy except her husband, who had watched her romance running out its pre-destined course with calm indifference. William's mother and the other members of the family, who felt they had been disgraced by the happenings at Lady Heathcote's and by the public admission of Caroline's liaison, wanted him to wash his hands of her. This, because of his genuine concern about her welfare, he refused to do, and so things dragged on for another two years. Then at last, worn out by her schizophrenic outbursts and the insistence of all the Lambs, he agreed that there would have to be a separation. Caroline was writing *Glenarvon*, in the mysterious way already described, with the object of telling the world how ill-used she had been. Byron, William, Lady Melbourne, almost everyone she knew was critisized. The only tangible result, however, apart from good business for the booksellers, was to alienate her in-laws and her husband still further.

Plans for the parting, therefore, went ahead. The lawyers received their instructions and drew up the formal deed of separation. When eventually the arrangements were complete, William left London for Brocket, intending to spend a quiet night there. However, clever, resourceful and unpredictable Caroline followed him down, arriving late at night when he was retiring, and made a last desperate plea for sympathy and understanding.

When on the following morning the attorneys came with the various papers to be signed a great surprise awaited them, for they found Caroline sitting on their client's knee, feeding him with thin slices of bread and butter! William waved the bundle of papers away and announced blithely that he and his wife were reconciled!

Byron's funeral cortège

Nine years passed and then, on a day in June 1824, a melancholy thing happened. Caroline and William were out driving, and as they emerged from the gates of Brocket Park they met a funeral cortège making its way slowly and solemnly along the road. William, on inquiry, learnt what his wife had already intuitively guessed. Byron, who had identified himself with the Greek struggle for independence, was dead and they were taking his body back to Newstead for burial.

Caroline, seeing the sombre procession of coaches pass by, was deeply affected. Old memories flooded back tumultuously and she returned to Brocket in a state of distress. Again her nerves, unable to withstand the slightest shock, went to pieces. In the weeks and months that followed there were stormy scenes, when she screamed abuse at people, galloped about on horseback like a tormented Valkyrie, and raved compulsively for hours on end. To remind herself of Byron she hung his portrait in her bedroom; to forget him she drugged herself with laudanum and drank brandy by the bottleful.

A year later, in 1825, she and her husband agreed to separate. William went to live in London; she stayed on at Brocket Hall, in the solitude of the lovely Hertfordshire park, forcing herself to be content with the company of her ailing son, Augustus, and her ageing father-in-law, Lord Melbourne, and with memories of the poetic genius whose advent into her life had brought first a delirium of happiness and then, when love was dead, disappointment, fury and a lingering sadness.

CHAPTER SEVENTEEN

LORD MELBOURNE—GUIDE, PHILOSOPHER AND FRIEND TO QUEEN VICTORIA

AFTER the death of Lord Byron, and the accidental meeting with his funeral cortège as it moved solemnly along the Great North Road, Lady Caroline's nervous condition, as we have seen, again deteriorated. Her relationship with the arch-apostle of romanticism and revolutionary liberalism had received its death-blow years earlier, but the memory of it, brief and unhappy though it had been, lived on in the recesses of her mind and heart. Ever since the scandal at Lady Heathcote's ball and the publication of the novel, *Glenarvon*, which pilloried so many people, society had made an outcast of her, yet she was too vital a person to idle away her days in the seclusion of Brocket, away from the main current of London life in which she had delighted to move and display her effervescent personality.

Brocket, of course, was by no means lacking in social life. Visitors from the nearby country houses were continually calling, and there were even occasions when the Lambs, both of hospitable disposition, threw a party. On one such occasion, in 1820, Caroline made a more than usually determined effort to rehabilitate herself in the eyes of at least her Hertfordshire neighbours. Eighty invitations were sent out and arrangements made for a sumptuous supper, but when the night came only ten people sat down to table. Caroline, moreover, had trouble not only with her guests but with her servants, who seldom stayed at the Hall for very long because of the constant scenes she created. Once when preparations were being made for a big party she was annoyed by something the butler did or said and, jumping on to the dining-room table, tried with raised voice and imperious gestures to deal with what she thought, quite wrongly, to be his insolence.

William, her long-suffering husband, still feeling responsible for her, still half in love with her, put up with her moods as best he could. The tragedy of the situation was intensified by the fact that the mental abnormality of their son, Augustus, had been declared incurable. William, therefore, absented himself from Brocket as much as possible, and in 1825 decided, finally and irrevocably, that the only solution of his marital affairs lay in a separation.

Caroline agreed to go to Paris, and a farewell ceremony then took place at which she conducted herself so admirably that everyone was touched—indeed, the butler whom she had antagonized was actually reduced to tears. William made her a generous allowance, but she proved totally incapable of managing her own affairs and within three months was back at Brocket, where she knew that the Lambs would care for her. In the autumn of 1827 she fell ill unexpectedly, and in January was moved to London, where, with William hovering near her bedside, she died. Despite all that he had endured he was deeply moved, and confessed later that Caroline " was to me more than anyone ever was or ever will be." That he meant what he said is borne out by the fact that he did not marry again.

Home Secretary

The death of William's father occurred in the same year that the gods, having finished their sport with Caroline, cut short her sad career. Melbourne, the first viscount, had survived his brilliant wife, Emily, by twelve years, and lived on six months after the death of his daughter-in-law, remaining to the end a shadowy nonentity. With his departure William inherited the title of second Viscount Melbourne, and soon afterwards found himself half-reluctantly treading the road to power and eminence as a Whig politician.

The first office of importance held by the new Lord Melbourne was that of home secretary, in the period 1830-4, when the voice of Britain's industrial workers was first making itself heard. The agitation for parliamentary reform and extension of the franchise was to some extent met by the Reform Bill of 1832, which gave the vote to people with certain property qualifications. But the propertyless proletariat, living in slums and forced to work long hours in " dark Satanic mills," was not satisfied and strove on with undiminished vigour for its rights. A development that worried Melbourne a great deal was the formation of trade unions, particularly in the industrial north. While resisting the proposal of some Cabinet colleagues to outlaw the movement, which he thought unnecessary, he became more amenable to their arguments when trade union activities spread to the countryside, in which, as a landowner, he had a vested interest.

Eventually he resolved on a compromise measure that had been suggested to him by the lawyers: an old Act of Parliament was revived, under which it had been an offence to administer secret oaths. When in March 1834 it was learnt that a newly formed trade union had administered such oaths as part of its admission ceremony several men were arrested and, after the travesty of a trial, sentenced to seven years' transportation. Melbourne, grossly misled by the local magistrates as to the characters of the condemned men, confirmed the sentences.

The affair of the Tolpuddle Martyrs nearly sparked off the revolution that everyone expected and feared. Monster parades marched down Whitehall, but Melbourne, taunted by the opposition critics for his irresolution, remained firm, and would not even accept a petition that tens of thousands had signed.

His name, therefore, will for ever be remembered as the " villain " of this historic episode, though the end of the story is entirely to his credit. Two years later, when his position in the Government was much stronger, he pardoned the Dorset labourers, who were allowed to leave Australia and return to their native land.

Prime minister

Political power appears to have meant little to Lord Melbourne, for he was under no financial compulsion to carve out a career for himself; in fact he disliked the incessant warfare of Parliament and would have much preferred to spend his days at Brocket, walking round the park with a gun under his arm or browsing in his well-stocked library. From a personal point of view it was probably a good thing that greatness and the cares of office were thrust upon him, for though many of his Brocket memories were wholly delightful others, particularly those associated with Caroline in her last days, caused nothing but pain.

Melbourne became prime minister for the first time in 1834, for the second time in 1835, and remained in office for a total period of seven years. The accession of young Queen Victoria in 1837 was the great turning point of his later career, for he found in her the stimulus to action that had hitherto been lacking. Victoria, then an ingenuous girl of eighteen who knew nothing of statecraft, roused his chivalrous instincts and gave him, for the first time, a sense of complete commitment to the nation's affairs. He did his best to be the wise, kindly and loyal counsellor. Victoria accepted his homage and advice willingly, and confided to her diary the belief that he was " a most truly honest, straightforward and noble-minded man . . .

there are not many like him in this world of deceit." It is not too much to say that they became sentimentally attached to one another. Other people were quick to notice their mutual admiration, trust and affection, and made many jokes about it. " I hope you are amused at the report of Lord Melbourne marrying the Queen," wrote a lady of the court to her friend; " for my part I have no objection." Every week a bouquet of flowers came from the Brocket gardens to grace the royal boudoir.

The romance, for it was no less, ended only when Victoria married her handsome hero, Prince Albert, in 1840; yet the friendship remained firm for many years, even after Melbourne had ceased to be prime minister and, in his late sixties, was living in the country— a recluse who watched from afar the colourful pageant in which he had once been a leading actor.

The last years

In the spring of 1842, just after he had retired from politics, Lord Melbourne's health deteriorated; he had a stroke and again the pattern of his life was altered. Friends and relatives rallied round him and kept him going for six years. His younger brother, Frederick, came with his wife to spend several months every year at Brocket; and his sister Emily often left her home at Panshanger to keep him company and help with the housekeeping. Whatever their faults, the Lambs were certainly a united family, and seldom defaulted on their obligations to one another.

Yet, inevitably, Melbourne tended to brood. With an open book on his knee he would stare out of the windows of the Hall to the lake and the spinneys of young trees on the opposite side. Walking round the spacious rooms he would be reminded of his mother, " a remarkable woman, but not chaste," of his wife Caroline and their imbecile son—all dead. His mind dwelt on the young queen, whom he had served faithfully but by whom he was no longer needed. He thought of Windsor Castle and Buckingham Palace and the times when his presence there had been not only welcome but a vital necessity. As he allowed these vivid memories to overwhelm him the old man's eyes would fill with tears.

The end came suddenly on November 25, 1848, on a day when the leaves were sere and the skies grey. He was buried in the churchyard of St. Etheldreda's, Hatfield, in a spot close to Caroline, whose remains had been interred there twenty years earlier.

LORD AND LADY PALMERSTON—THE LOVERS WHO MARRIED AT FIFTY

CHAPTER EIGHTEEN

THE Brocket estate, so much admired by Queen Victoria, had towards the end of Lord Melbourne's life been somewhat neglected. Reduced financial circumstances forced him to economize on maintenance and repair work, and failing health had in any case made him indifferent about such things. Without the help of relatives, and in particular of his sister Emily, not even the atmosphere of past affluence could have been preserved.

Since Melbourne's only son, Augustus, had predeceased his father by thirteen years, it was Emily who, in 1849, inherited the estate. She, too, loved Brocket—with its green vistas between the oaks and hornbeams, its cascading waterfall, and the Palladian bridge that the architect Paine had built. There as a child she had romped about in the open spaces of the park with her brothers and their circle of high-spirited friends.

Emily, born in 1787, was very much her mother's daughter, less well intellectually endowed but possessing the same social graces, the same scorn for conventional attitudes, the same vitality. She married her first husband, the fifth Earl Cowper of Panshanger, only a few weeks after her brother William and Caroline Ponsonby had, in 1805, entered into their ill-fated union. Cowper was a nobleman blessed with a great deal of worldly wealth, but with no outstanding natural abilities. He was by nature dull and stolid, yet the match was far from being a failure.

Their home life at Panshanger was typical of the period. They raised a family of children, had their extra-marital affairs and yet managed to maintain a show of family unity, respectability and harmonious living.

The true state of affairs, however, was revealed by a somewhat bizarre incident that occurred in the spring of 1818, when Emily's mother, Lady Melbourne, lay desperately ill.

Distinguished admirer

Emily had been summoned to her mother's bedside in order to

The west wing of Hatfield House as it is today.

The statue of Lord Salisbury outside the gates of Hatfield House, familiar to all who pass along the Great North Road, is the work of Sir George Frampton, the sculptor famous for two London works : the Edith Cavell memorial and Peter Pan (in Kensington Gardens). He has portrayed the third marquess seated in a chair brooding meditatively, as if over some perplexing problem of statesmanship or philosophy.

A sculptured bust by an unknown artist of Robert Arthur Talbot
Gascoyne-Cecil, third Marquess of Salisbury, born at Hatfield in 1830
and prime minister 1885-6, 1886-92, and 1895-1902.

The church of St. Etheldreda, Hatfield, in which Lord Melbourne and his wife, Lady Caroline Lamb, lie buried.

A peaceful scene at Lemsford, a village near Welwyn Garden City, which inspired the song " Nelly Dean," known all over the English-speaking world.

The old Great North Road wending its way through Lemsford village. It was here at the top of the hill that Lady Caroline Lamb met Byron's funeral cortège. Brocket Park lies on the right.

Lemsford mill as it is today. Formerly owned by a local firm of flour millers, it is now used as an engineering workshop. The thick layer of foam is caused by the presence of detergents in the River Lea.

Henry William Lamb, second Viscount Melbourne, a great Whig statesman, who became prime minister in 1834 and was for several years Queen Victoria's devoted friend and adviser. He lived at Brocket for many years.

Brocket Hall, acquired by Sir Matthew Lamb in 1746 and completely
rebuilt by the famous architect James Paine. It was here that the first
Lord and Lady Melbourne brought up their six children.

Sunshine among the trees in Brocket Park. Two ramblers are crossing the bridge, the balustrade of which can be seen.

A view of Brocket Hall across the artificial lake created by damming the River Lea, which flows through the park. It was on a festive occasion held at the Hall that William Lamb and Caroline Ponsonby first became acquainted.

discuss various matters of family interest. Among other things, Lady Melbourne tried to extract from Emily a promise that she would be " faithful and true " to an ardent admirer as gay and distinguished as her husband, Lord Cowper, was dull and ordinary. That admirer was Lord Palmerston, then in his middle thirties, a man marked out by destiny for high political office. What Emily thought of her mother's request we can only surmise, but her conduct remained outwardly unaffected. She continued to play the part of loyal wife and devoted mother, indulging her romantic fancies but taking care to avoid scandal.

Reading her letters, many of which have been published, we catch endearing glimpses of her attending to her children's illnesses, arranging the annual Panshanger ball, or driving over to Brocket Hall to see how her brother William and her sister-in-law Caroline were managing their affairs. All the Lambs came to regard Emily, as they had previously regarded Lady Melbourne, as the capable, shrewd yet charming head of the family, who watched over their fortunes, their health and their love-affairs with matronly care and affection.

William certainly had many reasons to be grateful to Emily, especially after 1837, when Queen Victoria succeeded to the throne and the most brilliant phase of his career was opening. These happenings coincided with a drama in Emily's own life, for it was in June 1837 that Cowper, her lack-lustre husband, died, leaving her free to think more seriously about the pleas that her mother had made nineteen years earlier.

The queen approves

Soon after becoming a widow Emily left the rambling, castellated Gothic house at Panshanger (demolished only in recent years) and went to live at the seaside. She relaxed, found solace in the change of scene, and forgot her cares, until suddenly, at about the time when she would have been making preparations for Christmas at Panshanger, she decided that she would go to live at Brocket with her widowed brother. From a practical point of view there was much to be said in favour of such an arrangement, though William was just then far more often in town than in the country.

Sentimentally, Emily was far more attached to Brocket Hall than to the grey, pretentious house that the Cowpers had built. Brocket was brighter, more elegant, full of the memories of people she had

F

loved in her childhood. She had been happy there as a young woman, radiant with health and beauty, and found she could be happy there in middle age, when she was the mother of a family and her good looks were fading. Lord Palmerston, too, liked Brocket and was often there, openly demonstrating the constancy of his affections and the honourableness of his intentions. In his eyes at least Emily's charms were as potent as ever.

Soon it became generally known that romance was in the air, and that they were destined for one another. People were amused, but no one could think of any impediment to the match, and most of their friends were genuinely in favour of it. Nevertheless, two years elapsed before the engagement between Lord Palmerston and Countess Cowper was officially announced. The queen, on hearing the news, passed it on to Prince Albert (whom she was to marry in the following year), adding that she fully agreed with their decision. " They are both of them about fifty," she wrote, " and I think they are quite right to marry, because Palmerston, since the death of his sisters, is quite alone in the world, and Lady Cowper is a very clever woman and much attached to him." Emily was also tiring of widowhood and thinking it was time she took steps to improve her "worldly position."

At last, on a bright, clear day in December 1839, the two were married at St. George's, Hanover Square, and—staid middle-aged couple that they were—lived happily together for the next twenty-five years.

Palmerston as prime minister

Palmerston's career had up to that point been interesting but not remarkable—though his intellectual capacity and energy had impressed everyone. Born in 1784, he had succeeded to the peerage as a young man of eighteen. When returned to Parliament for the first time in 1807 he had been a Tory, but later changed his ideas and became a Whig supporter. In 1818 he narrowly escaped death at the hands of a would-be assassin.

Twelve years later, in 1830, Palmerston was appointed foreign secretary, and while in that position pursued policies that often brought him into headlong collision with his Cabinet colleagues. In 1851 because of his premature recognition of the French emperor Napoleon III after the military *coup d'etat*, he was at the queen's peremptory request dismissed from office.

Time and public opinion, however, were very much on Palmerston's side, and soon he was back in political harness, as home secretary. He became prime minister for the second time in 1855, at a time of acute crisis. The Crimean war, the second China war (which resulted in the cession to Britain of Hong Kong), the Indian mutiny and the American civil war were among the major events of the historic period to which he belonged and which he helped to shape.

He was, of course, often at Brocket, relaxing there after his bellicose sword-crossings with the statesmen of other countries. In most of these encounters he came off best, and it required a Bismarck to out-bluff and defeat him—over the Schleswig-Holstein issue. But whether right or wrong, advancing or retreating, acting the part of liberal reformer or ruthless autocrat, he found in Lady Palmerston an unquestioning, resolute and constant ally.

When, on June 30, 1859, "Old Pam" formed his second administration he was already in the " sere and yellow leaf." Several years earlier Disraeli had dismissed him in contemptuous terms as " an impostor, utterly exhausted, and at the best only ginger-beer and not champagne, and now an old pantaloon, very deaf, very blind and with false teeth, which would fall out of his mouth when speaking if he did not hesitate and halt so much in his talk." He also suffered from gout, but that did not stop him from shooting pheasants or playing billiards.

In July 1865 Palmerston, aged eighty but still indomitable, fought his last election campaign and, notwithstanding his alleged infirmities and senility, was enthusiastically re-elected by his Tiverton constituents. The end, however, was very near, for in October of the same year, when the Palmerstons went down to stay at Brocket, he contracted a severe chill. For a day or two he hovered at death's door, but unexpectedly rallied. Lady Palmerston, writing to her son on October 16, 1865, reported that he had improved his diet, had eaten a mutton chop for breakfast and had taken a half glass of port besides. Two days later, surrounded by dispatch boxes full of state documents, and with his wife anxiously watching over him, he breathed his last.

Emily lived on for another four years, and still spent a great deal of her time in the gracious rose-pink mansion on the banks of the Lea that her ancestor Sir Matthew Lamb had built in the middle of the eighteenth century. No doubt she thought often of the people she had outlived—her brother William, her sister-in-law Caroline, her mother, her father, her two husbands, and innumerable friends. Only the Hall, the woodlands and the park—the incomparable natural heritage—remained as they had always been. The clear waters of the river sang endlessly under the arches of Paine's Palladian bridge; every evening the wildfowl swooped in formation before settling down on the artificial lake; in spring, as always, the flowers flamed in the gardens.

Emily lived on until 1869, enjoying the coming and going of the seasons, and when she too passed from the mortal scene she found a last resting place in Westminster Abbey, by the side of her distinguished second husband.

N.B. In October 1967 Brocket Hall became National Trust property.

CHAPTER NINETEEN

FUN OF THE FAIR

FOR the origin of fairs we must go back to medieval or even earlier times, when they were a means of bringing producers into contact with buyers. Indeed, the part played by fairs in stimulating commerce, both local and national, can hardly be exaggerated.

The association of the Church with commerce in medieval times may come as rather a surprise, but there is no doubt that it existed; in fact it was largely due to the fostering care of the abbots and bishops that the foundations of mercantile prosperity in our country were so truly laid. As an outstanding example of this may be mentioned the important role of the Cistercian abbeys in promoting the wool trade.

For many centuries fairs were held under the very walls of the church, and though this custom was declared illegal in 1285 suppression proved difficult, and it persisted to a much later date. Eventually, when expelled from the churchyard, the merchants and hucksters erected their booths in a circle round the cathedral or abbey. Often, as in the case of St. Albans, the abbey formed the nucleus round which not only the fair and the market but the entire city developed.

Barnet fair

The list of Hertfordshire towns that hold, or have held, annual fairs is a long one. Glancing over it one sees the names of Hemel Hempstead, Hertford, Bishop's Stortford, Stevenage and other places prominently featured. Barnet fair, still held annually in the early days of September, is the one that has achieved the greatest measure of renown. For the beginnings we have to go back 800 years—to the reign of Henry II, who founded the fair by means of a charter. Primarily it was as a cattle and horse fair that its name spread throughout the length and breadth of the land.

Even as late as mid-Victorian times Barnet fair was an important event. It continued to be so until 1868, when a disastrous murrain, or cattle disease, caused a major setback. With the construction of the Great Northern Railway the old site of the fair was cut in two and some of it permanently lost, but the fair continued to be of such size and splendour that in 1881 a *Daily Telegraph* reporter could still paint a picture of colourful confusion in the fields on either side of Barnet station. There is no reason to suspect him of journalistic licence when he described the whole as a " stirring spectacle."

" The high road in the vicinity of Barnet station," he wrote, " commands an uninterrupted view of the broad spread of hill and dale where thousands of horned cattle and horses are collected for buyers to pick and choose from, the cattle and horses being separate."

The horses, however, were the outstanding feature, the " big draw " for buyers, sellers and the general public. Horses were there from all parts of the British Isles: great droves of Irish horses and Scottish horses; hundreds of wild and unkempt Welsh mountain ponies; teams of sleek and powerful draught horses from the English shires. Foreign horses, too, were there, including a small Russian contingent.

Minstrels and acrobats

It was a kaleidoscopic scene, full of movement and dramatic incident. At any given moment dozens of horsebreakers might be seen engaged in fearsome combats with unruly steeds—the men pulling and swearing, the animals plunging madly, their teeth bared in menace, rearing up on their hind legs and " fighting with their fore feet." Scattered about in the meadow were commodious tents in which the judges—with solemn, equine faces—pondered their decisions!

Another writer, Father Bampfield, in his *Early Barnet Recollections* published in 1899, has left us a few fleeting impressions of the entertainments. There were, he records, all kinds of shows: a " marvellous theatre," Aunt Sallies, shooting galleries, minstrels and acrobats. Among other things, he watched from across a fence the " shying of coconuts," and saw the manageress of the booth knocked down by a clumsily thrown stick. One can well imagine the embarrassment of the worthy priest when he recognized the perpetrator of this uncouth deed as a member of his own church! However, despite much roughness and petty crime, he thought that the fair in 1899 was better than it had been in the days of his youth.

" But there was one delight of old times," he notes nostalgically, " which has now vanished—I speak of the races."

A major threat to the existence of Barnet fair came in 1888, when the lord of the manor petitioned Parliament for its abolition. Strenuous opposition was, of course, forthcoming from the towns-people, who maintained that their prosperity would be undermined by such action. Some 50,000 head of cattle, they pointed out to the home secretary, changed hands every year at the fair. Yet there were precedents enough to fortify the lord of the manor in believing that he could succeed.

St. Bartholomew's, in London, denounced by the citizens as an intolerable nuisance in 1855, had been abolished, and so had a number of other fairs; but Barnet residents were wholeheartedly in favour of their fair and so the hostile move against it failed. Building developments obliged it to move to a fresh site, but it continued, and still remains, very much a popular event. The horse fair, though gradually diminishing in importance, can still claim to be the high-light of the occasion, as it is attended by dealers from all over the country.

Pleasure fairs

Like everything else, human institutions are subject to the laws of evolution, and long before the end of the nineteenth century it was apparent that the old-fashioned fair, at which merchandise was bought and sold, had outgrown its usefulness; but, in altered form, and as a medium of display, it took on a fresh lease of life. The Prince Consort, in establishing the great exhibition of 1851, set the example for surveys, on a grand scale, of the nation's manufactures, arts and crafts. Pleasure fairs, branching off on their own, also began to develop along new lines.

In old books on Hertfordshire reference is made to pleasure fairs at Benington, Harpenden, Hitchin, Hoddesdon, Weston and other places, but there can be few towns and villages in the county that do not have a visit from a travelling fair in the summer season. The character of the entertainments has, of course, changed greatly since medieval times. Criminals are no longer hung, drawn and quartered to lend a touch of macabre excitement to the proceedings. There are no courts of piepowder, no miracle plays, no roasting of oxen, as in former days.

The pleasure fair as we know it depends on a few simple devices: coconut shies (with little opportunity of knocking out the lady in charge), games of chance, shooting ranges, roundabouts, swings, fortune tellers—and dodgem cars. The coloured wagons and cara-vans of the show people, the hurdy-gurdy music and the electric lights all help to create a happy-go-lucky, carefree atmosphere, but behind the façade of gay abandon is a prodigious amount of organization.

Gaudy, brash, uproarious and vulgar, the fairs yet seem to fulfil some fundamental human need. Certainly it may be said that they bring colour and gaiety to the countryside. They are social events, occasions for togetherness. Above all, the fairgrounds are places where young people, and even the not-so-young, can let off steam, release pent-up energies and, in general, have a good time in the open air with little harm to themselves or anyone else.

CHAPTER TWENTY

THE MERRY MONARCH AND NELL GWYNNE AT SALISBURY HALL

IT has been remarked of Charles II, restored to the English throne just over 300 years ago, that the details of his personal career were dwarfed by the great events—such as the Great Plague and the Great Fire—that occurred during his reign. Critics have commented that such successes as he achieved were due to the things he refrained from doing rather than to those he did! Others have denigrated him for his extravagance, cynicism and licentiousness.

Yet despite the detractors his image remains very much that of a tolerant, pleasure-loving monarch, anxious to heal the wounds left by the civil war and to avoid making the mistakes that had brought his father to the block. Foremost among his virtues were a lively, never-failing wit and the ability to enjoy a joke at his own expense. A hedonist in his way of living, he was also a lover of the fine arts and—witness his patronage of the Royal Society—of science.

Charles II, the " merry monarch," was by no means unacquainted with the Hertfordshire scene. Probably the association began in childhood, for Theobalds, the palace of James I at Cheshunt, had in due course passed to Charles I, who was living there in 1642 when the fratricidal strife between Cavaliers and Roundheads began. His son and eventual successor was then twelve years old.

Theobalds, a truly magnificent seat, was demolished by the Parliamentarians in a fury of ideological zeal and its treasures were dispersed. At the Restoration the manor of Theobalds became the property of Charles II, who promptly bestowed it on General Monk, the army commander who had been among those responsible for his recall from exile.

A moated manor house

We move now to London Colney, near St. Albans, and a moated Tudor-period manor house, Salisbury Hall, which the king may have owned, though there is no certainty about this. The house, part of which still stands, was built during the reign of Henry VIII by Sir John Cutts, Treasurer of England, who in the year of the

Spanish Armada was busily engaged in arming Hertfordshire to repel the expected invasion.

Somewhat later, in 1616, Salisbury Hall was owned and occupied by one Richard Cole, a man of staunch royalist sympathies, who constructed a number of secret passages and hiding places in the house. One of these recesses, according to the local tradition, was occupied for a time, after the battle of Worcester in 1651, by Charles II—or Prince Charles as he was then.

Nine years after the Restoration Salisbury Hall was tenanted by another royalist, Sir Jeremy Snow, a personal friend of the king. The latter came to the Hall accompanied by pretty, witty Nell Gwynne, the orange girl and actress who had won a very special place in the royal affections. There, in the heart of homely Hertfordshire, the king could forget the intrigues and cabals of the court of London and relax.

Several writers have suggested that Nell Gwynne's eldest son, Charles, was born at Salisbury Hall; others have embroidered the often-told tale of Nell's plot to win her boy a title. According to one version of the story she referred to him, in the hearing of his father, as " the little bastard."

When Charles protested at the use of the word she answered sharply: " Well, I have no better name to call him by! " The king thereupon promptly created his infant son Duke of St. Albans! Another and more dramatic version has it that Nell Gwynne held her infant son out of a window of the cottage she occupied (adjacent to Salisbury Hall) and threatened to let him fall into the deep waters of the moat unless the king gave him a title.

Though the romantic legend is willingly accepted by many people, in the interests of historical accuracy it has to be recorded that Nell Gwynne's eldest son, Charles, born in May 1670, was not created Duke of St. Albans until 1684, i.e. when he was fourteen years of age and long past the nursery stage of his career!

Another Hertfordshire nook much favoured by Charles and his charming mistress was at Tring Park, where Sir Henry Guy, clerk to the Treasury, had built himself a residence. Nell Gwynne's portrait by the famous painter Sir Peter Lely may still be seen there.

The Rye House Plot

Like other monarchs of the Stuart line, Charles II was harassed from time to time by money troubles. Not a few of these were attributable to his extravagant manner of living, others were the result of Parliament's reluctance to make the necessary financial provisions for running state affairs. Robert Clutterbuck, author of *The History and Antiquities of Hertfordshire*, has noted an interesting I.O.U. signed by Charles during the years of his exile. It reads: " I doe acknowledge to have received the summe of one hundred pounds sterling of J.F. which I doe promise to repay as soon as I am able. Bruges. 21st December 1657. Charles R."

The man who advanced the money was John Fothergill, of Rickmansworth, who after the Restoration was rewarded by being appointed sheriff of the county. It is not known where and when the loan was repaid.

Another learned Hertfordshire historian, Sir Henry Chauncy, reminds us that it was Charles II who by " letters patent, dated in November anno Regni fui, 1680 " granted that the borough of Hertford should be " a free borough of itself; and from thenceforth be and remain a free borough for ever."

Tolerant though he tried to be, Charles II did not lack enemies, and towards the end of his life, in 1683, an attempt was made to assassinate him and his brother. Among the plotters was a Hertfordshire man, Richard Rumbold, a maltster with a taste for political adventure. The plan was to waylay the king as he returned from Newmarket to London, and to commit the act of regicide at a Hoddesdon farm, Rye House, of which a few crumbling remains are still extant. There was at the same time a larger and more ambitious conspiracy afoot.

As it happened, the king left Newmarket a few days earlier than he had intended—due, it is said, to a fire at his lodgings—and the plotters' timetable was disrupted. An informer had also been at work, and everything was discovered by the king, who did not fail to mete out condign punishment to those involved in the plot.

Richard Rumbold, the ex-Cromwellian soldier, managed to escape to Holland and eluded the Stuart executioners for two years. He made the mistake, however, of returning to Scotland, where he was promptly arrested and brought to trial. Like so many of the other conspirators, real and imagined, he was found guilty and sentenced to death. One part of his quartered body was exhibited on the malting at Rye House as a token of the king's displeasure, and as a warning to the Whigs, religious dissenters and all others in Hertfordshire who might be toying with the idea of treason.

Nell's triumph

Something yet remains to be said about Mistress Gwynne—
" pretty, witty Nellie," as Pepys called her. She was born in 1650,
but whether her birthplace was Hereford or Drury Lane is a matter
for debate. Neither do we know definitely whether she was the
daughter of a " dilapidated soldier " or of a Covent Garden
fruiterer.

Her biography really begins at the point, shortly after the Restoration in 1660, when she was selling oranges in the pit of Drury Lane
theatre. Attracted by her youthful good looks and vivacity, a player
named Charles Hart gave her some training for the stage, and in
a very short time she was acting important parts in the plays of
John Dryden, then all the rage.

Nell Gwynne was particularly good at rendering risqué prologues
and epilogues, and it was during such a performance that, " wearing
a picture hat with the circumference of a coach wheel," she attracted
the attention of the king, who, as we know, was very fond of the
theatre—and of the ladies.

He carried her off to supper, and from that moment onwards Nell
Gwynne—" young, indiscreet, confident and of an agreeable
humour "—was to remain firmly fixed in the royal favour. She also
made heavy demands on the exchequer, and wheedled £60,000 out
of Charles in four years. On one occasion she paid £4,500 for a
pearl necklace, the property of Prince Rupert, which caught her
fancy.

With such extravagant tastes it is not surprising that Charles, as
he lay on his deathbed, should have been a little worried about her
future. Despite the counter-attractions of Lady Castlemaine and
other ladies of quality, he had been genuinely fond of her, and
almost his last words, addressed to his brother James, were " Let
not poor Nellie starve."

The king's worst fears came near to being fulfilled. Soon after
his death Nell had to melt down her plate, and later James, who
succeeded to the throne, had to enter £729 in the Secret Service
accounts to keep her out of Newgate jail for debt.

In 1687 Nell sickened and died " of an apoplexy "—after a short
and meteoric career of thirty-seven years. The pretty orange girl,
unable to read or write, had made her way, first as an actress, then
as the protégée of a great poet, and finally as the mistress of a king.
She had been instrumental in founding the Royal Hospital at

Chelsea for veteran soldiers—thus proving that she had a warm heart. At Salisbury Hall, as already related, she had forced Charles to acknowledge her son and ensure him an honoured position in society by creating him Duke of St. Albans, which clearly demonstrated her basic sense of responsibility and cleverness.

That dukedom was, indeed, a triumph of the first order, and only Nell Gwynne could have pulled it off. Certainly her story introduces a note of frivolous gaiety into the sober records of the county— but is that not to be welcomed rather then deplored?

CHAPTER TWENTY-ONE

HERTFORD—THE COUNTY TOWN

THERE are Hertfordshire towns with long, and even romantic, histories which have yet failed to preserve more than token traces of their original characters. Hertford, whatever else may be said against it, is not one of these. Critics fume because it has not developed, commercially or industrially, as it might have done. Stripling new towns, they point out, have overtaken it, leaving it dead and derelict by all modern standards.

That is undoubtedly one way of looking at Hertford; another is that the town, despite its proximity to London, has resisted the assaults and blandishments of the twentieth century with quite enviable success. Time has not actually passed it by, but in all essentials it remains what it has always been: the hub of an agricultural county, without pretentions to smartness or desire for hustle and speed. Hertford has managed to remain itself despite the coming of the banks and supermarkets, the automobile and the electricity grid.

" Conjecture, always busy in tracing out the origins of names which are hidden in the obscurity of years, has left many fanciful derivations of Hertford," writes Lewis Turnor in his excellent history. " According to some antiquarians, the proper orthography is Hartford, that is the ford of the harts "—to which we may add that the derivation, if not the orthography, is now accepted by almost everyone. Certainly Hertford, happily situated among forests at a point where four rivers meet and the waters are shallow, is easily imagined as a haunt of the wild deer.

The historical records go back some 1,300 years. A stone carefully preserved in the castle grounds informs us that at Hertford the East Saxon kings held a council or synod in A.D. 673, an event marked by much colourful pageantry. Little, however, is known about those far-off times, and Hertford's history does not really begin until the ninth century, when Alfred the Great was attempting to expel the warlike Danes from the land.

94

The status of a borough

It was in A.D. 894 that a Danish fleet succeeded in sailing up the River Lea as far as Ware, then no more than a tiny village. There the invaders decided to settle and build a strongpoint from which to attack and plunder the surrounding countryside. King Alfred, after rousing the citizens of London, pursued the enemy and, reaching Ware, forced them to fight. Success, however, eluded him on that occasion and he had to abandon the struggle for the time being.

The Danes then converted Ware into an armed camp and headquarters. Apart from throwing up defensive earthworks they constructed a weir across the Lea, and by increasing the depth of water in the river created a sizeable harbour for their ships. Hertford they pillaged, burnt and laid waste on several occasions. Those inhabitants who survived the raids were left in a desperate plight—until Alfred suddenly hit upon a stratagem that turned defeat into victory.

The Danes' lifeline was, of course, the Lea, along which their fleets passed virtually without interference as far as Port Hill, to the north of Hertford; and it was to the Lea, with its tidal waters, that Alfred turned his attention. His plan was a simple one: to cut the line of communication and leave the Danes at Ware stranded high and dry. First he diverted the course of the river at Waltham by dividing it into three separate channels. Next, by closing the sluice-gates at Blackwall, he kept the tidal waters out of the Lea, with the result that the Danish ships were soon put out of action. One by one they were attacked and destroyed. Finally, striking hard at Ware, the king drove the marauders out. The victory, which resulted in the capture of a vast amount of military equipment, proved decisive.

Unfortunately, Hertford had been so ruthlessly devastated that it was decades before the town resumed its former aspect. Alfred's son, Edward the Elder, was responsible for many of the new buildings that arose and for strengthening the earthworks and other defences. The same monarch conferred borough status on Hertford, which became part of the " king's revenue." Citizens received the title of " burgesses " and thenceforth enjoyed many privileges.

Royal charters

William the Conqueror placed Hertford, with the other English boroughs, on the same footing as the incorporated towns of France, which enjoyed many special immunities and rights. The town was confirmed in its licence to trade and to hold markets and fairs; it was granted the right to make its own by-laws and manage its own day-to-day affairs. William authorized the " corporation," as it was later called, to appoint a bailiff to collect the king's rents, tolls and customs, and a steward to sit as assessor to the bailiff in the borough courts.

A memorable moment came in 1553, when Queen Mary I granted the town a royal charter in which all the municipal privileges that had been conferred earlier were reaffirmed and a number of new ones added.

The borough was incorporated under the title of " the bailiff and burgesses of Hertford," and its liberties were fully detailed in the charter. Members of the corporation, whose number was limited to sixteen, were empowered to elect from among themselves the bailiff and to appoint constables and other officers. Three fairs were mentioned, falling on specified dates, and the corporation was permitted to establish pie-powder courts " to receive stallage, piccage, and all other profits, amercements, actions, commodities, and emoluments whatsoever, with all liberties and free customs appertaining to such fairs, paying 13s. 4d. to the queen for the three fairs at Michaelmas every year."

A second charter was granted to Hertford in the thirty-first year of Queen Elizabeth I's reign. This confirmed the town in all the " divers rights, jurisdictions, franchises, liberties and easements " which it had for long enjoyed. Furthermore, Elizabeth's charter established a constitution. The bailiff and burgesses were entitled to have a common seal, to build a jail, to seize the goods and chattels of felons and outlaws, to have a market once a week, on Saturday, and to hold an extra annual fair. The levy on the citizens was increased to £1/6/8/ per annum " in lieu of all rents and services."

In 1605 James I gave Hertford its third charter, declaring it a free borough to be incorporated as " the mayor, burgesses, and commonalty of the borough of Hertford," by which name it should have perpetual succession. On the feast of St. Michael the burgesses were to choose the mayor for the succeeding year, and provision was made for the appointment, in case of need, of a deputy.

King James's charter is an interesting document, but on the whole it did not do more than confirm Hertford in its long-established privileges as granted in the two previous charters.

Reproduced by courtesy of the National Portrait Gallery

The third Viscount Palmerston, one of England's most remarkable prime ministers, married Countess Cowper, née Emily Lamb, who in 1849 succeeded to the Brocket estate.

Paine's Palladian bridge, which, with its waterfall, is one of the most attractive features of Brocket Park.

Another view of the elegant Palladian bridge in Brocket Park. It was designed and constructed by the architect James Paine some 200 years ago.

The Lea at Waterend, near Wheathampstead, on the fringes of Brocket Park.

Caroline Lamb wrote her novel "Glenarvon" at Brocket Hall in mysterious circumstances, working by candlelight when everyone else was asleep. After the break with
Byron she made a bonfire of his letters in the grounds of the beautiful park.

Enjoying the fun of the fair at Welwyn Garden City.

Another Hertfordshire fair scene.

Reproduced by courtesy of R. B. Fleming and Co. Ltd.

King Charles II, who after his restoration in 1660 was, according to Macaulay, " more loved by the people than any of his predecessors had ever been." The portrait is by Sir Peter Lely, the famous court painter. With acknowledgments to the Librarian of the Royal Society.

Eleanor Gwynne (1651-87), the English actress who began her career at Drury Lane theatre as an orange-girl. She became the mistress of Charles II in 1669, and their relationship lasted until the king's death fifteen years later. He gave her Burford House at Windsor and humoured many wild extravagances. Nell is believed to have persuaded Charles to found Chelsea Hospital, which may help to explain the popularity she enjoyed with all classes of people throughout her life.

Salisbury Hall seen across the moat.

Nell Gwynne's Cottage, standing beside the moat at Salisbury Hall, London Colney.
It is believed that the first Duke of St. Albans, Eleanor Gwynne's first son by Charles II,
was born here. The story is told that she held her child out of a window and
threatened to drop him into the moat unless he was granted a title.

The County Hall, Hertford.

Rural crafts

The chronicle of Hertfordshire's county town, it will be seen, is long and varied—but, it may be asked, what of today? What of its future in an expanding, affluent society? These are questions to which only the briefest answers can be given.

Hertford, despite the challenge of its two go-ahead rivals, Watford and St. Albans, remains the administrative centre. From County Hall come the directives that, for example, bring the much-admired Hertfordshire schools, true fantasies of glass and steel, into being. The highways, the libraries, the fire stations and many other services are provided by the county council for a rapidly growing population.

Within easy reach of London, at the head of the once navigable Lea, Hertford has advantages that might have enabled it to develop from a " town of innkeepers " into an important centre of commerce and industry. However, it decided to evolve in an entirely different way, and rejected all those manifestations of progress it did not like. Commerce there is in Hertford, but on the retail rather than the wholesale scale.

There are as yet no mass-production factories. Hertford will, however, apologetically admit to a few engineering workshops, foundries and depots. Their impact has, however, yet to make itself felt in a big way, and they are regarded with something of the good-humoured tolerance of the countryman for all new-fangled things.

Hertford's most important building, in a symbolical sense, is perhaps the Corn Exchange, which stands in a main street not far from the Shire Hall, and reminds us that it is the capital of a county that is still very close to the land. The rural crafts of malting, brewing and flour-milling, and trades having some link with the farms and market-gardens are, and will probably long remain, the town's mainstay—and how very important those homely activities, concerned with the daily necessities of life, still are!

G

CHAPTER TWENTY-TWO

HERTFORD CASTLE

SO comparatively modern is the appearance of Hertford Castle that not until one comes to look at the crumbling, weather-beaten remains of the curtain wall—the " rude remains of high antiquity," to quote John Scott of Amwell—does it acquire any genuine interest.

The site, close to a ford over the Lea, was first fortified in Saxon times—possibly by Alfred the Great when fighting against the Danish invaders. At the time of the Norman Conquest there was already some kind of tower, of wood or stone, standing at the summit of an earthen mound and surrounded by a palisade, a moat and other defences. In fact, *c.* 1066 it was a castle of the motte-and-bailey type, such as are depicted in the Bayeux tapestry. William the Conqueror, who immediately took steps to strengthen the castle, appointed a Norman, Peter de Valoignes, to be its first governor.

A century or so after the Conquest the Angevin monarch Henry II decided that radical alterations were necessary to bring the ancient fortress into line with the latest military thinking. The work, on which he expended considerable sums of money, was begun in 1170 and three years later had advanced to the stage where it was possible for the garrison, consisting of a company of knights and men-at-arms, to move in.

Today nothing remains of the original Hertford castle with the exception of part of the flint-and-rubble wall, which in places is seven feet thick, a picturesque postern gate, the small artificial mound on which the keep stood, and scattered fragments of gates and guard-houses. The red-brick building in Jacobean style with which we are familiar dates back, in the main, no farther than the eighteenth century.

Medieval history

Castles were, of course, an important feature of the feudal system wherever it existed, and as far as this country is concerned their building and custodianship were very much a royal prerogative.

They served two main purposes in early times: they were the means by which the monarch dominated the surrounding countryside and strongholds from which he could direct operations against rebellious barons. Hertford appears to have been no exception to this general rule.

During the reign of King John the barons, for once, are to be observed in action as the upholders and champions of social justice. We see them resisting the tyranny of this masterful monarch, who, with cynical impartiality, robbed all sections of the community, whether rich or poor. Soon after his accession to the throne one Richard Montfichet was governor of Hertford Castle. A man of strong character and warlike disposition, he was allied to some of the most influential families in the land. When Montfichet joined the barons in their demands for redress of grievances the king deposed him and appointed Robert Fitzwalter in his place; but this baron was also drawn into the great confederacy and relinquished his office.

Fitzwalter, it is interesting to note, was one of the twenty-five " conservators " of Magna Charta, the historic document that compelled the king, grudgingly and in bad faith, to accept limitations on his power, which after the manner of medieval kings he had considered absolute.

As we know, hardly was the ink dry on Magna Charta, and the confederacy of the barons dissolved, than John revealed the treachery of his nature by denouncing it as a mere scrap of parchment, to which he had appended seal and signature under duress. Hertford Castle was then committed to the care of Walter de Godarvil, who converted it into a truly formidable bastion.

Meanwhile the barons had enlisted the aid of the dauphin of France in their struggle, and his armed forces, welcomed by the citizens of London, advanced upon Hertford and laid siege to the castle. Godarvil, loyal henchman of the discredited king, conducted its defence with remarkable skill and resource. When, after executing bloody carnage among the French forces, he was obliged to capitulate, the dauphin, in acknowledgment of his courage, allowed him to retain arms and horses.

Of the 300 years following the troubled reign of John, of the knightly tournaments held at Hertford amid scenes of great pomp and pageantry, of the many changes in the custodianship of the castle, and of the distinguished prisoners—among them King Bruce of Scotland and King John of France—it housed, it is impossible to write, for the subject matter is too great. We must press on to consider later episodes.

Maskings and mummeries

" On the accession of Henry VIII," Lewis Turnor tells us in his *History of Hertford*, " the castle presented a ruinous appearance, and seemed to be fast falling into decay." He goes on to attribute this state of affairs to the refusal of successive owners to undertake repairs, and to the ravages of the Wars of the Roses, which had contributed to neglect of property throughout the country.

Henry VIII, consumed with the same lust for power as John had been, but in other ways one of the more significant of the English kings, evinced a certain fondness for Hertfordshire, and as far as Hertford Castle was concerned made generous amends for the lack of interest shown by his predecessors. He had the building examined, and then allocated considerable sums for its restoration. The record of his expenditure, among other things, throws an interesting light on the relative values of money now and then.

Six or seven pounds, it was estimated in a contemporary account, would yearly keep the castle and the adjacent houses " staunch and dry." With the king in residence forty or fifty pounds would have to be added to that sum for the kitchen and other offices. But though the repairs and restorations were duly executed Henry VIII seldom visited Hertford Castle, and when he did so it was usually on his way to Hatfield or Hunsdon, where he had other and more favoured retreats.

His son, upright but consumptive Edward VI, spent his childhood years in Hatfield Palace, but on the death of his father in 1547 at once removed to Hertford Castle, where he was received by his uncle, later to become the Protector Somerset, and prepared for his coronation. Accompanied by Princess Elizabeth and a brilliant retinue of nobles, he was soon on his way to Enfield, and from there to Westminster, a frail and, one imagines, bewildered lad, for he was only nine years of age. His sister, later to become Queen Elizabeth, is believed to have been a frequent visitor to the castle, where " maskings, mummeries and sports " were arranged in her honour. Later, it may be remarked, she granted to the citizens of Hertford a charter confirming certain ancient privileges they had enjoyed.

It was at about this time, late in the sixteenth century, that the sessions of Parliament were held in the castle on several occasions while London suffered from the plague.

Oliver Cromwell

Almost every monarch from William the Conqueror to Elizabeth I—Richard Cœur de Lion is the notable exception—had been interested in Hertford Castle and had occupied it—if only for a few days to enjoy the pleasures of hawking and hunting. Its fall from royal favour occurred with the accession of James I to the English throne in 1603; in fact it was during his reign that most of the old buildings were demolished, leaving, apart from the " rude remains " already mentioned, only a sixteenth-century gatehouse of red brick. This gatehouse, much altered and rebuilt, forms the northern part of the building that we now know as Hertford Castle—the southern wing was added in the eighteenth century. According to the *Victoria County History* " all the windows as well as the pseudo-Gothic corbelling and the embattled parapet belong to that period."

As we have seen, James I had no use for Hertford Castle, for he was too much enamoured of his estate at Theobalds, near Cheshunt, and the fine palace he had acquired there. He made a grant of Hertford Castle and manor to his son Charles in 1609, leaving their management in the hands of trustees. The prince in due course, after his accession as king, granted the castle to William, the second Earl of Salisbury, of Hatfield, and in the hands of the Salisburys it has remained ever since.

Again we skip over the centuries, dismissing with a mere mention the sojourn of Oliver Cromwell within the walls of the castle—at a time when he was having trouble with the Levellers—and the various tenants, including Sir William Harrington and the Cowpers, who held it on lease and left their mark upon its architecture.

Early in the nineteenth century Hertford developed an interesting link with the East India Company, greatest of the old-time trading corporations, which virtually ruled the sub-continent of India for over 100 years. A veritable army of civil servants, officials and administrators was needed to cope with the gigantic tasks the company had assumed, and the court of directors decided to utilize Hertford Castle as a temporary training centre. There, within the seclusion of the crumbling Norman walls, on the banks of the " cerulean Lea," the seminary or college remained until, in April 1809, Haileybury was completed and the students were able to move into more suitable surroundings. Even so, for yet another eleven years the castle was used by the East India Company as a preparatory school to which the future legislators, governors and agents were sent to be instructed in the elements of classical and general learning.

Apotheosis

After the East India Company had vacated the castle it was again used as a private residence. The final transformation—indeed the apotheosis—came in 1911, when Lord Salisbury leased it to the corporation of Hertford for a peppercorn rental of 2/6 a year. The building was then converted into a block of municipal offices, and the grounds, covering an area of approximately eight acres, were laid out very attractively as a public park.

CHAPTER TWENTY-THREE

CROMWELL IN HERTFORDSHIRE

DURING the winter of 1642, just after the civil war had broken out, King Charles I, with a view to controlling the official affairs of the counties, appointed a number of sheriffs. In the case of Hertfordshire the choice fell on Thomas Coningsby, of North Mymms, a man who had served the king loyally but was unpopular because of the harsh way he had levied " ship money," as well as for other reasons.

A skirmish at St. Albans

On January 14, 1643, Coningsby, the royalist high sheriff, paid a visit to St. Albans with the object of making capital out of certain grievances that were agitating honest citizens all over the county. The times were unsettled, and they sought an end to the violence of " unruly and dissolute multitudes " who were threatening property and life.

Coningsby, with a brilliant retinue of Cavaliers, entered the city by way of Holywell Hill and, turning left, came to the historic market place. There he and his followers pulled up their horses and dismounted—in the space lying between the Red Lion inn and the Eleanor cross (which was then still standing). This unexpected appearance of the Cavaliers quickly brought the noisy bargaining between buyers and sellers to a close. A herald then stepped forward and, unrolling a parchment, called out in a loud, clear voice.

Like all proclamations, it proved to be a somewhat wordy affair and full of pompous phrases, but the gist of it must have been clear to all. King Charles declared that the disloyalty of Hertfordshire to his cause was attributable to the " malice, industry and importunity of certain disaffected and treasonous persons." These by threats, menaces and false information had led the inhabitants into rebellious acts. The herald went on to announce a free pardon for all offences committed prior to the proclamation and to warn those present against rendering assistance to the " army of rebels " in future.

After copies of the proclamation had been fixed in place on the market cross, Coningsby, with a view to winning support, spoke of plans to form Trained Bands (a kind of Home Guard) in the county, with the object of maintaining law and order and preserving the homes of citizens. It was an astute, though insincere, speech which might well have succeeded in its purpose but for the dramatic arrival of Oliver Cromwell on the scene.

Quite suddenly the space in front of the three inns—the Red Lion, Fleur de Lys and Christopher—were full of Roundhead soldiers. Captain Cromwell, who had by some means got wind of Coningsby's intentions, moved rapidly and resolutely into action. With six of his troopers he brusquely thrust aside the attendants guarding the sheriff and tore the proclamation down with his own hands. His attempt to arrest Coningsby, however, met with unexpected resistance, for the Cavaliers rallied round their leader and snatched him back from the rough hands of the dragoons.

Cromwell, determined to suppress the " new-made malignant high sheriff for Hertford," then gave the signal for twenty troopers on horseback to advance. For a time the unfortunate Coningsby was hustled backwards and forwards between friend and foe, but at last, with gold-and-silver-laced cloak torn to shreds and minus his feathers, he was taken prisoner. A final effort on the part of the Royalists to rescue him was easily beaten back.

Ultimatum from Royston

Cromwell at that time was a man of forty-three. After the indecisive battle of Edgehill, in 1642, he had worked with the eastern association, and spent much time in raising cavalry forces. These forces, to which Hertfordshire made its full contribution, were responsible for the victories at Marston Moor in 1644 and Naseby in the following year. Only two days before Naseby, Cromwell, with 1,000 horse and 3,000 foot, had been stationed in the Hitchin/Royston area. Men of the county took part in the battle, and after it the highways of Hertfordshire were crowded with Royalist prisoners, who were marched off to St. Albans, Hertford and other places.

We hear of Cromwell again in Hertfordshire; for example in 1647, during the second part of the civil war, when the Parliamentary army, consisting of about 20,000 men, was in dangerous mood because its pay was in arrear and its disbandment threatened. On that occasion Cromwell was at Royston, urging restraint on the mutinous troops.

On the afternoon of June 10, 1647, the army, still seething, was drawn up at a rendezvous at Taplow Heath, near Royston, in a meadow that commanded the junction of the two roads to London —one through Puckeridge, the other through St. Albans—and from there the angry Ironsides planned a march on the capital. Cromwell, from his headquarters at Royston, drew up a remarkable memorial letter to the Lord Mayor and aldermen of the City of London, stating the terms and conditions that would have to be complied with before his army would consent to be disbanded. On receipt of this letter from Cromwell Londoners were thrown into a state of " wildest commotion," as they believed he intended to march on the capital at once. The army actually moved forward on the following day from Royston to St. Albans, but there it was met by commissioners who came with promises that Parliament had been petitioned for its just demands to be granted in full. This placated the soldiers and the crisis was resolved.

Crushing the Levellers

Yet another dramatic incident in which Cromwell took part was the mutiny in Corkbush Field, near Ware, when he clashed with the Levellers—the democratic party in the English revolution, which had the support of the new model army, the yeoman farmers and the small traders.

At a spot near the source of the New River between Hertford and Ware part of the army assembled on November 15, 1647, and was later joined by the two " mutinous" regiments of Colonels Lilburne and Harrison, who had come to the rendezvous unbidden. These two regiments arrived on the scene in an intransigent mood, with papers stuck in their hats on which was the motto " England's freedom and soldiers' rights."

The Levellers have often been represented as wild and irresponsible revolutionaries, but it can now be seen that they were no more than radicals " born out of their due time "—liberal thinkers who advocated equal rights for men and women, colonial freedom, reform of unjust laws, abolition of the death penalty for petty crimes, the ending of imprisonment for debt, religious tolerance and the freedom of the press. These views, now universally accepted, were political dynamite in the seventeenth century, and Oliver Cromwell was determined that they and the Levellers should be suppressed.

When he arrived at Corkbush Field he was promptly presented

with a petition by one of the regiments, and a stormy scene began to unfold. At the centre of the turbulence was Lilburne's regiment, the leaders of which circulated the " agreement of the people " and made fiery speeches.

Cromwell, in stern mood, harangued the regiments to such good purpose that they eventually assured him of their loyalty. Only Lilburne's and Harrison's regiments remained obdurate and refused to take the mottoes from their hats. Enraged by their defiant attitude, Cromwell drew his sword and charged into the rebel ranks. When some of the loyal troops joined him in his attack the regiments wavered, gave in suddenly, and submitted to discipline.

A council of war then followed in Corkbush Field, and it was decided that some form of punishment should be meted out to the offenders. Eleven of the mutineers were made to step forward, and three of them received sentence of death. As an act of clemency, Cromwell conceded that only one of them need die, and he ordered the three to draw lots. The unlucky one, a man named Arnold, was placed at the head of the regiment and shot.

He lay a limp, defeated figure in Corkbush Field; yet it may be said that his spirit went marching on. Reforms gradually came, and today—three centuries later—it is clear that the cause for which he and the Levellers made a stand has on many essential points won through to victory.

CHAPTER TWENTY-FOUR

SIR HUGH MYDDLETON AND THE NEW RIVER

A scheme for drawing water from the River Lea, which rises in the Chilterns and after meandering through Hertfordshire joins the Thames below Blackwall, was first considered during the reign of Queen Elizabeth I. Engineering difficulties and considerations of cost had, however, discouraged execution of the plan, which was in many ways a most promising one. Not until many years later, when the problem of supplying London with water had become desperate, was it adopted and translated into reality.

The name permanently associated with the New River project is that of Sir Hugh Myddleton, who may be described as one of the city's earliest and greatest benefactors. Born in 1560, he left his home in North Wales when a young man and established himself in Basinghall Street, close to the Guildhall, London's ancient civic centre. After serving his apprenticeship to a goldsmith he turned to the related business of banking, and also engaged on a large scale in cloth-making and foreign trade.

Heavy expenditure

The Act of Parliament enabling the Corporation of London to implement the New River scheme was passed in 1605, during the reign of James I, who had given it his blessing and was later to support it financially. The essence of the project was to convey water to the city from Chadwell and Amwell in Hertfordshire by means of a thirty-eight-mile cutting or canal. Armed with the necessary legal authority to acquire land, the corporation was yet hesitant about taking the first practical steps in commencing the work, and three years after the parliamentary sanction had been granted nothing more than a survey had been carried out.

Hugh Myddleton, who takes the stage at this point, had long interested himself in the New River scheme, and, sensing that the corporation was inclined to abandon it because of the heavy expenditure involved, himself offered to shoulder the task. In March 1609 the common council took him at his word and transferred its powers to him, with the proviso that he should complete the undertaking within the next four years.

He threw himself heart and soul into the work, but ran into all kinds of difficulties. There was obstruction from the landowners, who demanded exorbitant compensation and raised objections of the most extravagant nature. The canal, they complained, would lead to flooding of their estates and convert the fields into bogs. They even petitioned Parliament to repeal the Act for bringing the New River to London, but, fortunately, Parliament was dissolved before the matter could be debated and when it reassembled in 1614 the work was finished.

The king helps

Though the opposition was overcome it did succeed in impeding Myddleton's progress, and he was obliged in 1611 to ask the Corporation of London to extend the agreed period of four years. At the same time, because of the drain on his limited personal resources, he ran into financial difficulties and, finding it impossible to carry on, applied to King James I for help.

The monarch was acquainted with Myddleton and knew something about the New River project, for he had an estate at Theobalds in Hertfordshire, and had been intrigued by the excavating operations. Myddleton's move was therefore extremely adroit, and the outcome was that James agreed to assist by taking over half of the entire enterprise.

Their understanding involved the payment to Myddleton of half of his outlay to that point and the acceptance by the king of half of all future costs. Any profits realized were to be equally shared, and though James wanted no part in the management he insisted—with characteristic Scots carefulness—on appointing a commissioner to audit the accounts.

By invoking the king's aid Myddleton surmounted his financial difficulties and there were other substantial gains. The landowners, impressed by the royal patronage, became suddenly more co-operative; and a rival scheme, for supplying the whole of London with water from the Lea at Hackney, was discouraged from proceeding further. Work on the New River was resumed and made rapid progress.

A royal charter

At last, on Michaelmas Day 1613, the great undertaking was

completed, and a ceremony took place—at a point not far from Sadler's Wells theatre in Rosebery Avenue—to celebrate the event. The Lord Mayor, Myddleton's own brother Thomas, presided over the proceedings, and many of the aldermen were there. A squad of workmen wearing green caps and armed with picks and shovels marched three times round the New River head; then, to an accompaniment of rolling drums and ringing church bells, the sluice gates were opened to allow water from Hertfordshire to gush into the Clerkenwell reservoir. It was a turning point in the history of London, which for the first time was assured of an adequate and wholesome water supply.

The cost—including the acquisition of land, cutting the river and building bridges—was never accurately ascertained, but according to some authorities was not far short of £500,000, a great sum of money in the early seventeenth century. Myddleton's whole private fortune was invested in the enterprise.

The famous joint stock company entitled " The Governor and Company of the New River brought from Chadwell and Amwell to London " was not, strangely enough, incorporated until after the capital construction had been brought to a close. The company enjoyed the privilege of a royal charter.

At the first meeting of the court of directors Myddleton was appointed governor, but he reaped little reward financially. Not, indeed, until after his death, which occurred in 1631, did the New River company pay its first modest dividend. However, there was consolation in the fact that in 1622 James created him a baronet.

Eventually, of course, the New River cutting did amply justify the money and the heroic endeavours involved in its construction. London, expanding all the time, had an insatiable thirst for water, and the company from about 1640 onwards enjoyed long spells of prosperity. Some of the adventurers who had partnered Myddleton lived long enough to pocket the higher dividends, and others, by selling out their shares at a profit, became " rich beyond the dreams of avarice."

A number of monuments to Myddleton, in acknowledgment of his work for the citizens of London, were subsequently raised at Chadwell and Amwell in Hertfordshire, at Islington Green, on Holborn Viaduct, and in the courtyard of the Royal Exchange— this last standing in the very heart of the city which he had served with such liberality. His New River company, in which the king acquired a fifty per cent share, survived for nearly 300 years—until, in fact, it became the subject of a takeover bid by the Metropolitan Water Board soon after the formation of that body early in the present century.

Altogether we are left with the impression of a man who worked for the welfare of the community; of a " private enterpriser " who had at all times a lively and highly commendable sense of duty to others.

CHAPTER TWENTY-FIVE

EAST INDIA COLLEGE, HAILEYBURY

FEW chapters in English history are more romantic or dramatic than the one in which the career of the East India Company is recorded. Receiving its charter from Queen Elizabeth I in 1600, it rose to dominate India, to rule over countless millions of native people, and to exploit incredible riches. Heavy as its responsibilities were, it was not, however, until the early part of the nineteenth century that any great thought was given to establishing a college for educating the administrators and executives upon whom it had to rely so greatly.

Only when expansion of the Indian empire had reached almost unmanageable proportions did the East India Company take the necessary action. A college in the hamlet of Hailey, a short bus ride from Hertford, was founded in 1805, and in the scale of its architecture the visitor will find ample evidence of the power and wealth of the once great corporation. The site was a convenient one, only nineteen miles from the Leadenhall Street headquarters, and covered an area of some sixty acres. On May 12, 1806, the foundation stone was laid by Charles Grant, who was a Member of Parliament and an East India Company director. William Wilkins, an architect steeped in the Greek tradition, was made responsible for the design and construction of the building.

The very fine south front of the college was built of Portland stone and is no less than 423 feet long. Three groups of columns of the Ionic order lend grace and dignity to the mighty façade, which, extremely impressive in itself, is but one of four sides, for Haileybury, like the colleges of Oxford and Cambridge, is built in the shape of a square, with the various offices and students' accommodation massed round a quadrangle of closely clipped grass. During the course of construction, in 1806, George III was pleased to grant the college a licence for a coat of arms. A set of regulations was drawn up in 1808 at the order of the directors, and in 1809 the college was ready for use. A number of students who had been temporarily housed in Hertford Castle at once took up residence.

The importance of Haileybury as a college and military seminary can hardly be overrated. When, in 1813, the East India Company was confirmed in its chartered privileges for a further term of years, specific mention of it was made in the Act of Parliament that was passed to give legal sanction to the company's position. Among other things this Act specified that it should not be lawful for the court of directors to appoint to the presidencies of Fort William, Fort St. George or Bombay any person in the capacity of a writer unless such person should have been duly entered at such college, and have resided there four terms according to the rules and regulations thereof, and should produce at the expiration of that time a certificate under the hand of the principal of the college testifying that he had for this space of four terms been a member of the college and conformed to the rules and regulations thereof.

This enactment had subsequently to be suspended because the vacancies for writers in the presidencies far exceeded the numbers of young men qualified by the stipulated four terms' residence.

Students were instructed by eminent professors—Robert Malthus, famed for his population theories, was one of them—and the subjects included classical literature, mathematics, natural philosophy, political economy, English law, and general history. Not unnaturally, a particular emphasis was laid upon the study of oriental languages. Haileybury men were called upon to acquire the elements of Persian in every case, and of Hindustani, Bengali or Sanskrit according to the presidencies to which in due course they were nominated by the court of directors. Arabic was also taught, and special prizes were awarded to those who could demonstrate their proficiency in its use. Details such as these make it clear that the East India Company at that time required its servants to be quite knowledgeable. Many of them were, indeed, men of the highest capacity and integrity. Others failed lamentably, once they reached India, in applying their abilities; a few actively abused the trust reposed in them and were responsible for some of the subsequent troubles.

As is well known, injudicious actions of the company's officials helped to touch off the Indian Mutiny, and it was a realization of the need for direct control of Indian affairs by the Crown that led to the cancellation of the Elizabethan charter. The rich, powerful and autocratic corporation, with hardly a compeer in the history of world commerce, which had maintained its own armies and fleets,

Hertford war memorial, designed by Sir Aston Webb. The life-size hart was executed from a model by Alfred Drury, R.A. The memorial, which stands in the centre of the town, was unveiled by the mayor of Hertford in 1921. Simple and yet inspiring, it now commemorates the dead of both world wars.

Hertford Castle.

The Norman wall at Hertford Castle.

The postern gate (early fourteenth century) and part of the curtain wall protecting Hertford Castle. The trees are planted in what was formerly the moat.

Hertford museum contains a fine collection of relics and curiosities of county interest.

An old malting by the riverside at Hertford.

This plaster work over a row of shops in Hertford dates back to the
sixteenth century.

Oliver Cromwell, who confronted the Levellers at Corkbush Field, near Ware.

St. Andrew's church, Hertford. In the interior is a tablet in memory of the
son of Thomas Dimsdale, a pioneer of anti-smallpox inoculation.

This memorial to Sir Hugh Myddleton and his "immortal work" was erected in 1800 at Great Amwell, one of Hertfordshire's most renowned beauty spots. Weeping willows droop their boughs over the water as it flows on its way to the capital.

was obliged, in 1859, to surrender its remaining privileges and to close its doors.

The East India College at Haileybury automatically ceased to function as a training centre for the company's personnel, and in 1862 it was converted into a public school.

H

CHAPTER TWENTY-SIX

THE STORY OF THOMAS DIMSDALE

The Quaker physician who became a baron of the Russian Empire

THE Dimsdales are a well-known and respected Hertford-shire family whose fame and fortune were founded in the eighteenth century by an ancestor who was a physician. Thomas Dimsdale, the son of John Dimsdale, of Theydon Garnon, Essex, a member of the Society of Friends and himself a doctor, received his medical training in London, at St. Thomas's Hospital, where he studied with exemplary zeal. The exact date when he set up his practice in Hertford is not known, but was probably in 1738, when he was twenty-four. He married for the first time in the follow-ing year. When his wife died, in 1744, Dimsdale took a dislike to Hertford and, as a volunteer surgeon, joined the army that George II was raising to crush the Scottish rebellion of 1745. On his return to Hertford Dimsdale married for the second time, the lady being the daughter of John Iles and a relative of his first wife. His financial circumstances were then so good that he was able to abandon the practice for many years, and it was not until 1761, when his family responsibilities had grown, that he resumed where he had left off.

One of the most cruel and persistent scourges then afflicting mankind, second only in importance to the plague, was smallpox, outbreaks of which were constantly recurring. Dimsdale, seeing the ravages, personal and social, caused by the disease, was troubled, and tried hard to find a way of mitigating it and reducing its truly frightening toll. He began studying, and in 1767 published a treatise, *The Present Method of Inoculating for the Smallpox*, which was immediately recognized as an outstanding contribution to the literature on the subject. Copies of the work, which ran into several editions, found their way abroad, and in 1768 the author was in-vited to St. Petersburg, then the capital of Russia, to inoculate the empress, Catherine the Great, and her son, the Grand Duke Paul.

Catherine appears to have had complete faith in Dimsdale and in his method of preventing smallpox, but there were others in Russia, as there were in England, who believed that it was " flying in the face of providence " to infect a healthy person with the virus of a malignant disease. The story, therefore, goes that Catherine organized relays of post-horses between St. Petersburg and the nearest border town, so that if anything went wrong Dimsdale was assured of a rapid escape route.

Inoculating the nobility

These precautions proved, of course, to be quite unnecessary. The inoculations were a complete success, and Dimsdale, instead of being forced to flee in disgrace with a price on his head, was loaded with honours. Catherine created him a councillor of state, with the hereditary title of baron, and gave him a large sum of money—£10,000, with an additional £2,000 for expenses. Further, the empress granted him a life annuity of £500 and the right to include in his family arms a black wing of the spread eagle of the imperial Russian arms in a gold shield placed in the centre, with the customary helmet on a shield adorned with the baronial coronet. The patent, or open letter conferring the title, incorporated a portrait of Catherine, and eventually found its way to Camfield Place, Essendon, home of the later Dimsdales, where it was treasured as the memento of a great adventure.

Dimsdale, the first baron, visited Russia again in 1784 to inoculate the Grand Duke Alexander and his brother Constantine. Again he was most graciously received by the empress, who, it may be remarked, survived her own inoculation by twenty-eight years and lived to be acclaimed as one of the greatest rulers that Russia has ever had.

Dimsdale's fame spread all over Europe, and brought him into contact with several other heads of state and royal personages. While still in Russia—and Catherine would have liked him to stay there—he visited Moscow, where he inoculated members of the nobility and leading citizens, as well as their children. On the return journey from his first expedition in 1768 Dimsdale called on Frederick the Great at the Potsdam palace of Sans Souci, and was most hospitably entertained; and on the return journey from the second visit to Russia, in 1784, he passed through Vienna and had an audience with the Holy Roman Emperor Joseph II; but he was not called upon to render professional services on either of these occasions.

M.P. for Hertford

The last fifteen years of Dimsdale's long working life were spent in Hertford, where he had firmly taken root. That he was well thought of by the citizens is evidenced by the fact that for the ten years 1780-90 he was their elected parliamentary representative. Believing that charity begins at home, he opened an " inoculation house " in Hertford, to which people of all classes in search of immunity from the greatest killer of the age could go. This " clinic," as we would now call it, was under his own personal supervision.

Patients, it should be explained, were actually infected with a mild form of the disease. This method was, of course, later replaced by that of Edward Jenner (1749-1823), the discoverer of vaccination. It was in 1796 that Jenner made his first experiment with a cowpox vaccine, and since it proved a success the earlier method advocated by Dr. Dimsdale, which was not without its hazards, fell into disuse.

When his wife died in 1779, leaving him with a family of seven, Dimsdale married for the third time, and lived on to the ripe old age of eighty-eight. He was buried by the side of his ancestors at Bishop's Stortford, in the Quaker burial ground. A white marble monument in St. Andrew's church, Hertford, perpetuates the memory of this benevolent baron whose work did so much to advance the health and happiness of his contemporaries both at home and abroad. Posterity, too, has reason to be grateful for his efforts, which were of a truly pioneering nature.

CHAPTER TWENTY-SEVEN

SAMUEL WHITBREAD—ZEALOUS ADVOCATE OF THE OPPRESSED

THE approach to Essendon from the north side is winding and in places precipitous. At the bottom of the hill, close to the River Lea, a picturesque mill house drowses among the immemorial trees. On the way to the summit one passes through some of the most delightful countryside in Hertfordshire—well cultivated, leafy and lush. At the top of the hill, overlooking a triangular green, is the church of St. Mary the Virgin, which has associations with a remarkable man, Samuel Whitbread the younger, who devoted himself to the cause of social reform at a time when life was short and brutish because of disease, and many cruel and illogical laws were still in force.

Evidence of this may be found on an outside wall of Essendon church in the form of a tablet which records the hanging of a young man at Hertford in 1785 for theft. Such harsh retributions were a commonplace in Whitbread's day. Indeed, some 200 crimes could be punished by death, and had the sentences invariably been carried out there would have been mass executions all over the country and periodic decimation of the population. In practice the majority of those convicted and sentenced were reprieved. This, though it tempered the severity of the law and nullified its more ferocious workings, created anomalies of the most unjust kind, since the lives of the convicted depended entirely on the whims and humours of the judges. The reform of the criminal law was a matter in which Samuel Whitbread was deeply interested, and he was a warm supporter of his friend Samuel Romilly, a lawyer, who fought gallantly, though with little success, to abolish hanging for stealing and other minor offences. Whitbread himself is best remembered as an advocate of Poor Law reform, education for the children of working people, and abolition of the slave trade.

Bedwell Park

Samuel Whitbread senior, a London brewer, had sent his son to be educated at Eton, Oxford and Cambridge, and was himself a

man of humane conviction and a radical. Shortly after his marriage
to Elizabeth Grey in 1788 Whitbread junior, a very handsome man,
became interested in politics, and in the following year made an
onslaught on Pitt's government for its alleged waste of money on
military preparations. In fact, he developed into the most forceful
and respected speaker of the Whig opposition. Towards the end of
1795, when there was great distress in the countryside, he sponsored
a Bill to fix the minimum, as well as the maximum, wages for agricultural labourers, but was defeated. His Poor Law Bill, another
humanitarian measure, introduced in 1807, met with a similar fate.
Despite these rebuffs he struggled on fearlessly, attacking injustices
and abuses of all kinds.

A part of Samuel's childhood and youth were spent at Bedwell
Park, a little to the south of Essendon, though the record of his
doings there—even after the publication in 1967 of Mr. Roger
Fulford's biography—is full of blanks. The *Victoria County History*
states briefly that " Bedwell seems to have passed through many
hands. From the descendants of Richard Wynne it passed by sale
to Samuel Whitbread "—meaning, of course, Whitbread the elder.
The date of the acquisition of the fine Hertfordshire estate, only
twenty miles from the Chiswell Street brewery, was 1765, when the
future " advocate of the oppressed " was hardly out of the cradle.

Bedwell, a grandiose red-brick building, now occupied by the
Royal Victoria Patriotic School, was in a dilapidated condition
when the Whitbread family took up residence there, but the brewer,
with ample means at his disposal, soon made it habitable and fit to
receive any visitors who might turn up. Though many of the local
gentry were inclined to look down their noses at a man employed in
the liquor trade others were quite willing to be friendly, and Mr.
Whitbread could therefore always rely on the presence of a few
stylish guests, from nearby Panshanger or even Hatfield House, at
his parties. Young Samuel spent his last Christmas at Bedwell in
1787, grumbling about the excess of " mince pies and prayers " and
impatiently waiting for the day when he could wed the young
woman with whom he was in love.

Woolmers

The sister of Charles (later Earl) Grey, who was to steer the great
Reform Bill of 1832 through Parliament, Elizabeth Grey was
inclined to be self-centred, but there was no doubting either her

intelligence or her beauty. Whitbread had been friendly with Charles Grey at both Eton and Cambridge and it was through Charles that he and Elizabeth had become acquainted. The marriage took place in January 1788, at Fallodon, and after a short stay in London bride and bridegroom went to live at Woolmers, located at only a short distance from the Bedwell estate. Their new home stood in the centre of a pleasant park, which gave Bess plenty of scope for developing her recognized skill as a gardener. A curious feature of Woolmer Park was the " Acherley Hole," a sheet of water some seventy feet long and forty feet wide, but of—apparently—unfathomable depth. In rainy weather it overflowed into the Lea and at other times dried up.

The married life of the Whitbreads at Woolmers was happy—though Samuel complained of the lack of local interest in fox hunting—and they lived in that part of Hertfordshire for twelve years; until, in fact, 1800, when they moved into the adjoining county of Bedfordshire after disposing of their property.

Bedwell Park had been sold in 1796, shortly after the death of Whitbread's father. The old man, in a codicil to his will, bequeathed to St. Mary's church, Essendon, the sum of £533/6/8, producing £14/10/- a year, of which £5 was payable to the rector for administering the sacrament at least eight times a year and the residue in distribution of bread to the poor of the village. It was an act of piety and conscience-salving philanthropy typical both of the man and of the age.

Inside St. Mary's the visitor may inspect a much-admired Wedgwood font—made of basalt, a kind of black porcelain—given to the church by Miss Whitbread, one of the elder Whitbread's two daughters.

Eloquent tribute

Samuel Whitbread the younger's career ended dramatically, and was linked by a strange chance with one of London's oldest and best-loved theatres. In 1809 fire gutted Drury Lane, in which Sheridan, brilliant creator of *The School for Scandal*, was the principal shareholder. Whitbread helped the unlucky playwright to rebuild the theatre, a generous action which explains the presence of Whitbread's bust in the foyer to the present day. Unfortunately, the high hopes placed in the future of the new theatre were not realized, and some friends who on Whitbread's recommendation had put money into the venture were badly hit by the non-payment of a dividend. This, it is believed, worried him to such an extent as to unbalance his mind and plunge him into a state of morbid depression. The aftermath of the Napoleonic wars with its miseries may also have added to his distress. Whatever the truth may be, it was just after Waterloo, in July 1815, at the age of fifty-one, that he committed suicide. His death, still in many ways inexplicable, shocked not only his friends but even the enemies who had most bitterly opposed him and his liberal policies.

Whitbread had, of course, his human faults. Lord Byron denigrated him scornfully as " the Demosthenes of bad taste and vulgar vehemence "—a reference to his forthright parliamentary speeches —and others decried him for his vanity. Yet there were thousands, from the Prince Regent down to the humblest cottager at Essendon, who mourned his passing. Romilly, his friend, probably expressed the general feeling when he declared that he had been " the promoter of every liberal scheme for improving the condition of mankind, the zealous advocate of the oppressed, and the opposer of every species of corruption."

Nothing need be added to that eloquent and just tribute, except the reminder that many of the social reforms for which Whitbread had fought so courageously were, long before the end of the nineteenth century, triumphantly achieved. Slavery was finally abolished, the criminal laws were relaxed, and the State made itself responsible for educating the workers' children. So far, therefore, from Whitbread having been a somewhat tiresome champion of lost causes it is clear that the exact opposite was the case.

CHAPTER TWENTY-EIGHT

SPORTING INNS

THERE is little interest today in blood sports, or in entertainments that involve cruelty to animals or birds. Anyone who cares to visit a Hertfordshire inn will find only the most harmless forms of amusement available. Apart from good cheer, a hospitable atmosphere and genial company, there may be little more than a game of darts or shove-ha'penny.

The position in former days was rather different. Innkeepers were then expected not only to provide liquid refreshment for their customers but to satisfy their sporting instincts. The diversions most in favour often did involve practices barbarously cruel; for example there was the old English sport of " dog and duck," often pursued where the inn happened to be near a pond.

A duck, with its wings pinioned so that it could not fly, was placed on the water and pursued by hungry dogs. Usually the innkeeper provided the duck and the customers brought the dogs. Naturally there was a great deal of excitement, and bets were made on the result. When the duck, by skilful manœuvring and diving, succeeded in eluding the dog the dog's owner paid for drinks all round. Should a dog catch the duck drinks were on the house.

Inns bearing the sign Dog and Duck were once common in the London area. At Hitchin will be found a Dog and at Burnham Green a Duck, but whether they were venues for the kind of sport described, and popular as recently as 100 years ago, is uncertain.

Bull-baiting was another sport formerly practised in the neighbourhood of the larger inns. A bull, the more ferocious the better, was tethered by chain to a post in the inn yard. Dogs of a special breed were then unleashed to harry the bull. Bear-baiting was conducted on similar lines. Cock-fighting, a very old and spectacular form of sport, was patronized by commoners and kings for hundreds of years. Falconry and archery, once practised in the gardens attached to country inns, were nobler forms of sport.

With the advance to a more humane society the old and savage customs of tormenting animals for pleasure were declared illegal, but reminders of them are still scattered about the countryside in the shape of inn signs. Though Bull and Dog and Dog and Bear are probably unknown in Hertfordshire, there is no lack of Bulls (e.g. Wheathampstead, Stanborough and Royston), Broxbourne has a White Bear, and there are Falcons at St. Albans, Cheshunt and Watford. The Fighting Cocks at St. Albans is perhaps the most famous of these inns with sporting associations or sporting signs. Picturesquely situated at the foot of Abbey Mill Lane, it was undoubtedly a cock-fighting centre at one period of its history, but it is believed to have been used in medieval times by the monks of St. Albans as a fishing lodge.

Because the name of Izaak Walton is inseparably linked with Hertfordshire one would have expected to see, especially on the banks of the Lea, some Fishermen's Arms, but they are in fact conspicuous by their absence. The Jolly Fishermen, a McMullen's house, is to be found at St. Margaret's, there are Fishery inns at Boxmoor and Aldenham, and at Watford there is an Anglers inn. Other names may, however, need adding to the list.

Very much to our modern liking is the game of cricket. This, too, though it cannot trace its descent back to classical antiquity as bull- and bear-baiting can, has behind it an interesting history. Though its origin is obscure, it was played as far back as the thirteenth century; the first cricket club was formed at Hambledon, Hampshire, in 1750. Marylebone Cricket Club came into being thirty or forty years later. Established on Thomas Lord's cricket ground in Dorset Square, it moved to St. John's Wood in 1814, and has remained there ever since. Cricketing inns are, of course, to be found everywhere, the most famous being Lord's Tavern, which formerly stood on Lord's cricket ground. In Hertfordshire we have Cricketers at Redbourn, Harpenden, Hitchin and other places. The Benington Cricketers is notable for its vigorously painted sign showing batsman and wicket-keeper in action.

Skittles is another game that was played with great gusto at many inns and public-houses not so long ago. Indeed, up to 1918 skittle alleys were attached to at least half of those in the country. A bowling green adjacent to an inn or public-house is, on the other hand, a combination all too rare, but there is one at the Cherry Tree, Welwyn Garden City, and another at the Three Horse Shoes, Norton. There, during the summer months, the players (both men and women) emulate Sir Francis Drake and disport themselves in careless rapture on fine greens of Cumberland turf.

The Fox and Hounds at **Rickmansworth** and Hunsdon, the Greyhound at Aldbury and St. Ippolyts, the Hare and Hounds at St. Albans and the Sportsman at Croxley Green are a few more names, chosen at random, that will evoke vivid images of activities encouraged, sponsored or sustained by the country inns.

CHAPTER TWENTY-NINE

DIAMOND MAGNATES AT TEWIN

ON the banks of the Mimram at Tewin stands a 150-year-old mansion which, though architecturally dull and hardly mentioned in the county histories, has many interesting associations. In a guide to Hertfordshire published in 1880 it is referred to as " a charming seat . . . called Tewin Water, wherein lived and died Henry Cowper, a fine old English gentleman. . . . The pretty little park . . . is singularly umbrageous, being thickly wooded, and the River Mimram is expanded into a serpentine sheet of water in front of the mansion." The description is as valid today as ever, for the scene has hardly changed.

Built by the Cowper family in about 1800, Tewin Water became the property, towards the end of the century, of Alfred Beit, a German financier, and it is with him and his younger brother, Sir Otto Beit, and not with the " fine old English gentleman," that these brief reminiscences are concerned.

The father of the two Beits was a Hamburg merchant who, though of Jewish origin, had adopted the Lutheran faith. He placed his son Alfred, at the age of seventeen, with a Hamburg firm that had South African interests, and there the young man gained much useful experience. After spending a year in Amsterdam, where he worked in the diamond trade, Alfred sailed for Cape Town and on arrival at once trekked inland.

Kimberley, to which he went, had been founded in 1871, only four years earlier. The town, about 100 miles from Bloemfontein in Cape Province, was named after the first Earl of Kimberley, who when Secretary of State for the Colonies had placed the newly discovered mines under British protection. Young Beit, accurately assessing the potentialities of the situation, borrowed £2,000 from his father with which to break away from the firm he represented and set up his own business. He became a diamond merchant and, foreseeing future developments, bought up a considerable tract of vacant land, on which he built corrugated-iron offices which, in the prevailing circumstances, he was able to let at high rents. At a later date he sold the ground at a fabulous profit.

Associate of Cecil Rhodes

Though it has been said that Beit was not a speculator, this early Kimberley transaction was at least a most successful business transaction, even when it is remembered that fortunes were at that time being made with comparative ease. There are stories, indeed, of " diggers " going out after a shower of rain and picking up diamonds as if they were mushrooms—by the basketful! Beit was lucky, though he had certainly shown initiative in being on the spot at the right moment and in seizing his opportunity.

While at Kimberley, Beit struck up a friendship with Cecil Rhodes, the young man from Bishop's Stortford whose name was to be indelibly written into South African history. Rhodes was, of course, an empire-builder of the old-fashioned type. He had come to dream of British interests extending to the tropics and beyond, of a Cape to Cairo railway and other grandiose projects. Largely responsible for the annexation of Bechuanaland in 1885, he went on to form the British South Africa Company, which occupied Mashonaland and Matabeleland, thus forming Rhodesia. Beit, though of German origin, shared many of these imperialistic ideas and aspirations.

He had in 1882 entered into partnership with J. Porgius and Julius Wernher, and six years later sailed for England, as he had decided to make London his business headquarters. In 1890 the firm of Wernher and Beit was set up, and it was about then that he acquired the house in Park Lane and the Tewin Water estate.

Rand goldfields

Something yet remains to be recorded of Alfred Beit's life in South Africa and of the contributory sources of the great fortune that he left. In 1888 he visited the goldfields of the Rand, and there repeated his Kimberley tactics by buying up land. As this included some of the best outcrop mines it quickly acquired a value far in excess of the purchase price. Beit, it should be added, played a leading role in developing the Rand goldfields. In particular he applied considerable capital to advancing the Great Deep Level Scheme, which formed the basis of the territory's future prosperity.

Like Rhodes, Beit was a bachelor. When he died in 1906, at

Tewin Water, he was survived by his mother, two sisters and a younger brother.

Benefactions

While the majority of people in the world are faced with the problem of making money the very wealthy man's problem is what to do with the surplus after his personal needs—often surprisingly simple—have been satisfied. Alfred Beit, like other millionaires, bought works of art and acquired many of the status symbols, such as the Hertfordshire country house, appropriate to his station in life. Like other men with the Midas touch, he had been much criticized and was fully aware that excessive wealth brings at least some measure of social disapproval. He had been the object of hatred and envy, and in the end decided to dispose of a considerable portion of his fortune by princely acts of philanthropy. Other wealthy men both before and after him have done that, but seldom on a more munificent scale.

In actual fact, after providing for friends and relatives, he made bequests amounting in total to £2,000,000 to various public institutions—educational, medical and charitable—in which he was interested. The Imperial College of Technology, Guy's Hospital and the National Gallery were the chief London beneficiaries. Other money went to South Africa for the Cape to Cairo railway project and to his native Hamburg for charitable purposes. The residue of his estate he left to his brother Otto, who was also charged with the task of administering the philanthropic trust funds.

Sir Otto Beit

Born at Altona, Germany, in 1865, Otto had come to England in 1888 and was naturalized as a British subject. Following in the footsteps of his brother, whom he greatly admired, he entered a London finance house with South African connections. When Alfred died in 1906 he succeeded not only to a great part of his brother's fortune but to the Hertfordshire country house. In fact, he lived at Tewin Water for the remainder of his life, and when he died in 1930 was buried, as his brother had been, among the rude forefathers of the hamlet in Tewin churchyard.

There are still people in the Mimram valley who remember Sir Otto Beit as a man who, though he entertained lavishly, had comparatively simple tastes. A story still in circulation concerns his gardeners, who were chosen, it is said, not so much for their gardening skill as for their prowess as cricketers! As a result the Tewin cricket team was exceptionally strong and able to give a good account of itself in various parts of the county.

Sir Otto—he was knighted in 1920 and became first baronet four years later—was himself of a philanthropic disposition. He too made munificent donations to the Imperial College of Technology, and was the founder of the Beit Memorial Fellowship for medical research. In 1897 he married Lilian Carter, the daughter of an American industrialist, and they had four children—two sons, the elder of whom succeeded to the baronetcy, and two daughters.

A new purpose

The Tewin Water mansion, it may be mentioned in conclusion, now serves as a home for partially deaf children, run by the Hertford-shire County Council. Many changes have been made to adapt the building for that purpose, and there have been extensions—yet the " charming seat " remains very much as it was a century and a half ago. The park, still " singularly umbrageous and thickly wooded," is particularly delightful in the springtime, when the willows are first bursting into leaf on the banks of the meandering Mimram and the daffodils are out.

CHAPTER THIRTY

SIR EBENEZER HOWARD AND THE NEW TOWNS

THE basic principles behind the new towns are widely understood and accepted, but who nowadays gives more than a passing thought to the man whose patient labours started the whole movement off?

The pioneer was, of course, Sir Ebenezer Howard, O.B.E., born in 1850. His parents were middle-class tradespeople in the City of London and their son started his life as a shorthand writer. After a trip to the U.S.A. he returned to England in 1879, married, and joined the staff of a firm of official parliamentary reporters. It was a job with small rewards, and Howard remained to the end of his days comparatively poor.

A Londoner born and bred, he was one of those who saw the folly of allowing the great octopus to spread its tentacles over the countryside. More than that, he was convinced that civilization could go forward only on the basis of co-operation. He believed that men should work on the principle of service to the community and not of self-interest.

Out of these two basic ideas emerged the dream of the garden cities. He wrote his famous book *Garden Cities of Tomorrow* and—not without difficulty—managed to get it published. It makes interesting reading even today, when so much is taken for granted. His plan for the ideal town was highly original. A marriage of town and country, it was to be constructed in the form of a series of concentric cirles, with the civic buildings at the hub. Between centre and circumference was to be a grand boulevard, 400 feet in width, planted with grass verges and trees. The shopping centre, or rather shopping circle, he suggested should be a glass-covered arcade, a " crystal palace " providing shelter from wind and rain and equidistant from all parts. There was provision for industrial and residential zones, for a light railway along the perimeter, and for playing fields. Six great avenues were to radiate from the centre, and the whole town was to be surrounded by a permanent agricultural belt.

The very quintessence of his scheme was that the new towns were to function as completely self-contained units, where people would work as well as live. They were not to be mere dormitory suburbs. Further, he put forward the revolutionary proposal that the community was to be sole landlord.

Shortly after the publication of his book Letchworth was begun —a bold experiment that was described as Utopian, but which proved itself in practice. In 1920 Welwyn Garden City was founded and is today a thriving town of 40,000 inhabitants. After World War II Stevenage, Hemel Hempstead and Hatfield were developed along similar lines, with resounding success. Every year town planners from all over the world come to see and admire them, and draw inspiration from the example they have set. Though the voice of criticism has not been entirely silent, there is little doubt that they have vindicated Howard's ideas. The speculations and dreams of 1898 are seen, in the Hertfordshire new towns, to have become reality. Not, of course, that the community-owned town of concentric zones has yet come into being—that still lies far off in the future.

Howard was a very likeable man, personally unambitious, an absent-minded philosopher and true philanthropist whose sympathies were with the masses, with the ordinary people aspiring to a home and a place in the sun for themselves and their children. Though lacking in the arts of showmanship he was a persuasive speaker and knew how to communicate his own unshakable faith to others. He had many friends and supporters, and his family life was happy.

Official recognition for the great work he had done came in 1927, when he was knighted. He died in the following year.

CHAPTER THIRTY-ONE

A BRIEF HISTORY OF DIGSWELL HOUSE

THE village of Digswell, pleasantly situated in the Mimram valley, can trace its history back for at least 900 years. Just after the Norman Conquest in 1066 Geoffrey de Mandeville received a grant of land in the district. Two centuries later the parish may have been quite populous, for in 1278 Lawrence de St. Michel applied to Henry III for a charter permitting both weekly and annual fairs to be held. Quite abruptly, probably after the ravages of the Black Death, the population dwindled, and in 1428 there remained only some half a dozen householders in the parish. The Mimram valley sank into a reposeful sleep from which it was not to be roused for nearly 500 years.

" A commodious mansion "

Early in the eighteenth century an old manor house—inhabited by the families of Perient, Horsey, Sedley and Shallcross—stood a little to the west of present-day Digswell House, at the end of Monk's Walk, a magnificent avenue of lime trees, which had to be cut down only a few years ago. This manor house, dour and weather-beaten, was purchased in 1785 or 1786 by George Nassau Clavering Cowper, third Earl Cowper, who died three years later and was succeeded by his eldest son. The Cowpers were not only one of the wealthiest families in central Hertfordshire, but included a poet, William Cowper, famous for *John Gilpin*, in their ranks.

When Digswell manor house was demolished in 1805 it was a Cowper—the Hon. Edward Spencer—who built the splendid new mansion with the history of which we are now concerned. Erected a little to eastward of the site on which its predecessor had stood, it was a commodious country gentleman's home, built in an archi-tectural style that can best be described as " neo-classical." A portico, with four massive columns, on the south front is its most impressive external feature.

Cussans, in his *History of Hertfordshire*, published in the 1870s and 1880s, tells us that the Hon. Edward Spencer lived in Digswell House for several years after its completion in 1806. In the decades that followed it became the residence of Sir James Mansfield, Sir John Norton, Thomas Powney Martin and others, who made few, if any, structural alterations or additions. More recently the house was used, at least temporarily, as a school and an office block.

When the seventh and last Earl Cowper died without an heir the estate passed to Lady Desborough, his niece.

An auction sale

During World War I Digswell House played an honourable role in serving as a hospital and nursing home for wounded Australian officers. Many were restored to good health in its peaceful surroundings, but seventy-three died there and these have their permanent memorial in the twelfth-century church of St. John, which stands very near to the house.

Shortly after the war, in May 1919, Digswell House, placed on the market by Lord Desborough for sale by auction, was acquired by Sir Ebenezer Howard—pioneer of the town-planning movement in this country—and a group of interested friends on behalf of the Welwyn Garden City Company, which, however, was not formed until the following year.

Sir Ebenezer Howard's copy of the auction sale prospectus, dated May 30, 1919, is still extant, and makes interesting reading. Digswell House (lot 12) is described as " an attractive residential property extending to an area of about 190 acres." After expatiating on the compactness of the estate, its exceptional advantages and its pleasant setting in " extensive woodlands, arable and pasture land " the auctioneer concludes his preliminary puff on the following note: " The residence occupies an excellent position on raised ground. . . . It is a substantial structure, with an imposing elevation, and commands good views over well-timbered undulating lands. The accommodation is spacious and well arranged over two floors."

In the following paragraphs brief descriptions are given of the lofty lounge hall, the drawing room, the library, the dining room, the billiard room, the eight principal bed and dressing rooms and the domestic offices, which included a butler's pantry, a large kitchen and a servants' hall—with the then ultra-modern conveniences of hot and cold water and electric light everywhere laid on!

We learn, turning over the pages, that the water supply in 1919 was obtained from a nearby Digswell spring, the water being raised by means of a water-wheel to storage tanks placed in the roof of the residence. Close to the house were adequate stabling quarters, with a coach-house, a coachman's cottage and a blacksmith's forge. Finally, mention is made of a gardener's " bothy."

The catalogue, though dull as all such compilations are, manages to convey most vividly the atmosphere of an age—stately, slow-moving, aristocratic—that is now vanished and gone beyond recall.

The Conference House

After Welwyn Garden City Company took over Digswell House no one knew what to do with it; in fact it became very much a white elephant. People loved visiting it at weekends. They loved sitting on the lawn in the shade of a fine cedar of Lebanon and, above all, they enjoyed watching cricket being played on one of the most delightful grounds in the county. But Digswell House lay in an area on the northern boundary of the garden city planned for late development, and until that development took place it had to justify its existence and earn its keep. This posed a difficult problem, and while it was being studied the house was rather neglected. Yet one of the most useful periods of its history lay immediately ahead.

Several public-spirited people, concerned about the future of Digswell House, began to turn various projects over in their minds, and eventually concluded that it might well be used for holding conferences—more especially those of an educational nature. The scheme was approved by the directors of Welwyn Garden City Company, and in 1928 a resident warden was appointed. A lively house-warming party was held and the first student conference took place only a few weeks later.

The innovation turned out to be a great success. Digswell House —only twenty miles from London and yet in the heart of unspoilt countryside—was in continuous demand, and between 1928 and 1939, when World War II broke out, some 500 conferences were held under its roof. The most varied organizations—religious, political, cultural—made use of it and, having done so once, came again and again. Every topic under the sun was discussed, from the sublime to the ridiculous, and those who came to talk or listen were drawn from every sector of society. Hospitality was extended to many foreign visitors.

Among the more famous guests of the Conference House (as it came to be called) were George Bernard Shaw, Paul Robeson,

Jimmy Maxton, Lord Beaverbrook and Hugh Gaitskell, men prominent in the arts, literature and politics. At the height of this phase in its career Digswell House was accommodating 3,000 visitors annually. The charge for a weekend—starting with Saturday tea and finishing with Monday morning breakfast—was fifteen shillings!

An artists' workshop

As we have seen, Digswell House was originally a nobleman's residence and later functioned as a school, as a hospital, and as a meeting place for the compulsive talkers and listeners. The final transformation came in the 1950s, by which time the pioneer Welwyn Garden City Company had been superseded by the development corporation, a statutory body. Again the question of what to do with the " commodious and desirable residence " arose.

It was Mr. J. E. McComb, then general manager of the development corporation, who suggested the idea of converting it into a " little Montmarte or Chelsea "—a place in which a group of artists could work and live in reasonable freedom and without having to worry too much about the grocery bills. This plan was accepted and, after the house had been repaired and renovated, six young artists, all under thirty, took possession. The group was financed and governed by the specially formed Digswell Arts Trust, which not only commissioned work from the artists but assumed responsibility for sales. Further, these young men who found homes and studios at Digswell were charged only nominal rents. The experiment, believed to be unique in England, got off to a good start, and in 1959 Countess Mountbatten of Burma officially opened Digswell House as an art centre.

Nine years later, in 1968, it is still serving that purpose. The number of artists has increased to thirteen, among them being a weaver, a print-maker and a stained-glass artist. One day—who knows?—Digswell may startle the world by producing a real genius.

CHAPTER THIRTY-TWO

WELWYN GARDEN CITY

IT was in 1920 that an elderly man, with an obvious attachment to Hertfordshire, first prospected the site on which the second, and perhaps most successful, of the new towns was to arise. Around him rolled miles of undulating countryside, the boundaries stretching from Welwyn and Digswell in the north to Hatfield in the south, from Lemsford and Brocket in the west to Panshanger in the east. Apart from a few farmsteads, a cottage or two and the converging railway lines there were few signs of human life. The area was well wooded; small rivers, the Lea and the Mimram, serpentined along two of its boundaries and nearly all that lay between was agricultural land valued at some £40 an acre.

Only a year or two after that preliminary survey by Sir Ebenezer Howard work on the proposed garden city had begun, and the first of the factories and houses had been erected and a railway station built. Despite many difficulties—for the start on Welwyn Garden City was made in the hard years following World War I—progress in the 1920s was continuous and on a worth-while scale. By 1928, the year in which the " father of the new towns " died, the outlines of the central part of the town had taken shape. The plan was beginning to become apparent; industry and population were settling down in the meadows, among the hornbeams and the newly planted rows of poplar trees.

In a geographical sense Welwyn Garden City was fortunate, for its position in central Hertfordshire, straddling one of the main railway lines, was ideal. The distance from London, twenty-one miles, was sufficient to ensure a rural environment without acting as a deterrent to the dweller in the " great wen " contemplating a change. To these advantages were allied others that had not been available when Letchworth was being built. The Government, for example, compelled to grapple with a gigantic housing problem, had in 1921 passed an Act granting the company then responsible for development substantial financial aid.

On the other hand, there were new and unfavourable factors, such as those produced in the early thirties by the world-wide economic depression, which retarded the growth of the town if only because it applied the brake to the establishment of the new industries on which the livelihood of the townspeople was largely to depend.

However, the work proceeded steadily if slowly, and by 1933 a number of factories, some small, some large, were in full swing, producing a variety of consumer goods such as wireless sets, pharmaceutical chemicals, grinding wheels and abrasives, processed foodstuffs, plastic moulding powders and electrical appliances. A film studio was producing films, and a famous racing motorist, Sir Henry Birkin, maintained a " stud " of Bentley cars in two of the Broadwater Road sectional factories. By the time that World War II broke out in 1939 the population was estimated at 18,000, a majority of the residents being young people.

By then, of course, a town hall, schools, a community centre and a department store had risen from the fields. The town had a cinema which could be quickly converted into a theatre and was, in fact, leased to the organizers of the Welwyn drama festival for one week in the summer of each year. A picturesque barn in Handside Lane was placed at the disposal of the thriving amateur dramatic groups. Clubs and societies existed in considerable numbers, catering for the sports enthusiasts, the craftsmen, the literary folk and the debaters. The only thing lacking was a cemetery, but this hardly mattered, since it was claimed that no one ever died there!

On the whole, therefore, it can be said that despite many difficulties the progress made in the first twenty years of Welwyn Garden City's existence was satisfactory—and it must always be remembered that it was progress to a well-defined plan.

Almost immediately after the declaration of war in 1939 civilian building work was brought to a standstill, but because several large London firms, including Imperial Chemical Industries, decided to use Welwyn Garden City as an evacuation base for staff its population was greatly increased; and, of course, once the local factories had been geared to the war effort thousands of incoming workers aggravated the congestion still further. Eventually many of the migrants returned to London and elsewhere, but a proportion, having found local employment of a permanent nature, decided to stay. When the war terminated in 1945 the problem that faced the urban district council and the company planners was no ordinary one.

But important changes were imminent in the ownership of Welwyn Garden City, and control passed out of the company's hands. In January 1947 Mr. Lewis Silkin, then Minister of Town and Country Planning, notified the parties concerned that he intended taking over. In due course a development corporation was formed and an outline plan and programme for the future was prepared and published. Building progress, at first hampered by material and labour shortages, was later speeded up and within a few years Welwyn Garden City was growing rapidly. Today ninety industries are located in the town, the shopping and commerical centres are virtually complete, and the population statistics are rising fast towards the aim of 40,000—more than double the pre-war figure.

What would Sir Ebenezer Howard think of it all if he were to revisit the scene of his first solitary excursion over the fields? No doubt there is much that he would deplore or even condemn outright. Of other things, including the general development of the town, it is probable that he would approve. Certainly he would be delighted by the aspect of the public gardens now that they have matured, and by the preservation to a great extent of the natural amenities, including many fine old trees. He could hardly fail to be gratified by the obvious efforts that have been made to adhere to the early plans.

Samuel Whitbread the younger (1764-1815). This fine portrait was painted by Sir Joshua Reynolds and admirably suggests the combination of shrewd businessman, staunch radical reformer and generous philanthropist.

The church of St. Mary, Essendon. On an outside wall of the tower is a tablet which records the hanging of a young man in 1785 for theft. Inside the church is an interesting Wedgwood font made of basalt.

Bedwell, a grandiose red-brick building, was purchased by Samuel Whitbread the elder
in 1765 and occupied by him until his death thirty years later.

The 150-year-old mansion at Tewin Water that was formerly the home of Sir Alfred
and Sir Otto Beit, diamond magnates, associates of Cecil Rhodes and philanthropists.

Tewin church and churchyard, in which Sir Alfred and Sir Otto Beit lie buried.

Digswell House, completed in 1806, has been used as a private residence, a conference house, a hospital, a school and an office block. It is now used as a residence by a group of artists.

The Fighting Cocks, Abbey Mill Lane, St. Albans, which claims to be the oldest licensed house in the country. It was undoubtedly a cock-fighting centre in former days.

Lombardy poplars, so prominent in the landscapes of the Netherlands and northern France, have also become characteristic of some English scenes. This view of a residential district in Welwyn Garden City shows what harmonious visual relations can be established between groups of houses and poplar trees.

Digswell viaduct, a masterpiece of railway architecture, was completed in 1850, and still carries main-line traffic to the north.

Sir Ebenezer Howard, garden city pioneer. By courtesy of the Commission for the New Towns.

A striking modern sculpture of a mother and child in Stevenage
new town centre.

CHAPTER THIRTY-THREE

BRASSEY BUILDS THE VIADUCT

THIS is the story—rough, tough and inspiring—of Digswell viaduct, one of the finest examples of railway architecture in the country. Six thousand men laboured and endured incredible hardships to bring it into being.

Few spots in central Hertfordshire retain more natural charm than the Mimram valley, which extends from Welwyn in the west to Hertingfordbury in the east. The hills, though they do not rise to any great height, are green and rolling. Between them flows a tiny river, rippling its way past stately homes and neat cottages. Even the Victorian railway builders must have been enchanted by the Mimram valley, though it posed for them a problem of no ordinary kind.

Twenty-four miles north of London, and nearly a mile wide, it had to be spanned if the Great Northern Railway, first projected in the 1840s, was ever to become reality. Critics of the scheme pointed out that the bed of the valley was little better than a water-logged swamp, and that there would be no foundations on which to build a bridge. Better to make a wide detour or abandon the idea of a railway from London to the north altogether.

However, the promoters were determined to surmount the " impassable barrier " as it was called. Digswell viaduct, one of the seven wonders of Hertfordshire, was begun and, thanks very largely to the energy and organizing ability of one man, was completed in just over two years.

The prince of contractors

Thomas Brassey, the son of a Cheshire farmer, had little education, but rose through sheer ability to become a highly successful railway contractor. Passing from one project to the next, and riding on the crest of the great Victorian railway boom, he eventually had interests in every part of the globe. The parliamentary Bill to establish a through line from London to York was passed—against fierce opposition—in 1846, and shortly afterwards E. Denison, chairman of the Great Northern Railway, enlisted the services of Thomas Brassey on a four-year contract. The building of Digswell viaduct turned out to be one of the major achievements of his life.

Brassey's methods were simple but thorough. There were, of course, no tractors, bulldozers, earth-moving machines or motor-lorries in those days. Only manpower, cheap and plentiful, was available. Under Brassey's direction an army of 5,000 navvies was marshalled and set to work digging foundations for the huge structure that was to leap across the valley and carry the iron road on its back.

Working with pick and shovel, the men dug an enormous trench 2,000 feet long, 300 feet wide and 100 feet deep. Spurred on by Brassey's demonic will and passion for speed, they toiled heroically through all the daylight hours, and even at night by the garish light of naphthalene flares. Thousands of tons of earth and saturated clay were dug from the valley bed, loaded into barrows, and dragged away by horses. At last, when the work of excavation was finished, mountainous loads of burnt clay and mortar were packed into the trench as a " grout," forming, as its builder had intended, a firm and indestructible base.

Monumental grandeur

Then began the colossal building task. Five million bricks, made on the spot of Hertfordshire clay, were needed before the fantastic bridge, designed on the lines of a Roman aqueduct, rose above the marshy meadows and over the treetops in complete and monumental grandeur. It has forty arches, each with a span of forty feet. The overall length, including the approaches, is 2,000 feet.

Endless difficulties were experienced while the constructional work was in progress, not least being the heavy frosts in the winter of 1849-50, but all were overcome, and so, little more than two years after the start, Brassey and his " navigators " could regard their work in its entirety, and they saw that it was good. Out of their unremitting toil had come something unique and inspiring—a masterpiece in brick.

The official opening of Digswell viaduct took place on August 8, 1850. Among the passengers in the first train to cross was a man named George Hudson, later castigated by Carlyle as " the big, swollen gambler " but then still enjoying renown as the " railway king." Hudson, for reasons of his own, had spent a fortune in endeavouring to stop the building of the Great Northern line. He had ridiculed the proposals for a viaduct, which he regarded as an impossible undertaking. When, obstinately, the Great Northern directors had declared their intention of going ahead he had predicted that they would lose every penny of their capital.

No doubt Hudson was furious with Brassey on that day in August 1850, but he could hardly have failed to be impressed as he looked down from his carriage window across the parapet of the viaduct into the lush green heart of the valley.

Knights of the shovel

How the 6,000 workers lived during the years that the viaduct and the Welwyn tunnels were being constructed is in itself an epic story. A great encampment was built to accommodate them—a shanty town, extending over a wide area, in which conditions must by any modern standards have been appalling.

The men—rough " knights of the shovel and pick "—ate and slept in tarred-canvas shacks. Exposed to all weathers, labouring like serfs and cut off from their womenfolk, they spent their leisure hours in drinking and fighting. Every Friday night they provided a brutal entertainment for the inhabitants of Digswell with their bare-knuckle fights. These were held at the back of an inn on the hillside at Burnham Green, The Duck, and the pugilists—for a small purse or a bottle of gin—would batter one another into insensibility. A bricklayer on the viaduct, Tom Sayers, attained championship status, and fought battles that are still spoken of with bated breath.

Engaged on a magnificent creative work in building the viaduct, these men were compelled to endure hardships and accept conditions which today would almost certainly start a revolution; yet for Brassey the men seem to have had the highest regard. They not only respected him but liked him, and in token of their appreciation presented him with a silver shield. This shield he displayed at the great exhibition held in Hyde Park in 1851—the year after work on the viaduct was finished.

Queen Victoria

A story, entertaining but apocryphal, still often told in Digswell on a winter's evening concerns Queen Victoria, who travelling northward on the Great Northern Railway for the first time was allegedly overcome by an attack of feminine nerves. Doubtful whether the viaduct would bear the weight or take the strain of a locomotive and carriages hurtling forward at high speed, she refused to be taken over!

The train was therefore stopped just short of the viaduct on the London side, and the queen, accompanied by friends and officials, dismounted and crossed the muddy, mile-wide Mimram valley on foot! Breathless but safe, she rejoined the train—which had meantime steamed to the other end of the viaduct—at a point now occupied by Welwyn North station.

The story is amusing, but was almost certainly invented—probably over the ale tankards at the Cowper's Arms, Digswell, the great contractor's headquarters—long after Queen Victoria's day.

CHAPTER THIRTY-FOUR

HOLDING FAST THE HERITAGE

We live at a time when great changes are taking place; when parts of the county—e.g. Barnet—have been wrested away and merged into the Greater London area; when, because of the building of new towns and the expansion of old ones, the countryside is dwindling in size and assuming an entirely new aspect. All this, of course, is a result of the population explosion, which has affected the counties of south-eastern England with particular severity.

Though there is probably no way of reversing this trend, much can be done, and must be done, to prevent the creation of more " subtopias " than already exist. Municipal authorities, no less than private individuals, have a right and a duty to demand that all new housing estates should be orderly and well planned, that industrial development is controlled, and that the historic monuments and buildings in which the county is particularly rich should not be left to the tender mercies of the vandals and the philistines who place monetary values high above æsthetic ones.

There appears at the moment to be only one body exclusively concerned with preserving Hertfordshire's inheritance from the past, safeguarding the rural amenities and combating the would-be despoilers of natural beauty. The Hertfordshire Society, which incorporates the Hertfordshire branch of the Council for the Preservation of Rural England, was formed in 1936 to co-ordinate all those varied interests having the general welfare of the county at heart. The objects of the society, which deserve to be more widely known, are as follows:

> To promote the general good of all inhabitants of the county of Hertford by stimulating and guiding public opinion in the preservation of the countryside and features of artistic, historical or local interest in all towns and villages.

> To prevent harmful disfigurement and to assist in the control of future development by relating preservation and enhancement of beauty to developments that must be provided for.

To co-operate in the development of agriculture and rural industries and their co-relation to rural life.

To promote co-operation between local authorities, town and regional planning committees, other societies, owners of property and all other persons interested.

To refer to, and discuss with, the relevant authority or organization all such inquiries as are conducive to the welfare of the social life of the county.

What the society has in practice done to implement these aims and objects is to establish an alert and vigilant " watchdog " organization throughout the county. It is, of course, the body responsible for initiating the best-kept-village competition, an annual event that attracts lively public attention. From time to time it has made representations in appropriate quarters to ensure that only qualified architects are employed to design new buildings and housing estates. It has prevented the demolition of old cottages and reminded local authorities of their powers, under the Housing Acts, to approve grants in aid for building reconstruction and renovation. It has exerted its influence to prevent the indiscriminate destruction of hedgerows and trees and to secure new plantings when felling and uprooting are unavoidable. Finally, the Hertfordshire Society has played a commendable role in enforcing the prohibition of unsightly advertisements in the rural areas.

These are activities that no one who cares about the past, present or future of the county can fail to be in sympathy with and support. Indeed, encouragement for, and participation in, such work is very much a matter of self-interest, for if we allow our environment to be wantonly destroyed we may as well abandon all hopes of gracious living for ourselves or our children and grandchildren.

The heritage of the past is ours to enjoy—the stately homes, the ruined castles, the art treasures, the churches, the inns, the green and pleasant land—and enjoy them we do. Everyone with a sense of responsibility, however, will be mindful of the fact that we are in the position not only of legatees but of custodians and trustees for the future.

BIBLIOGRAPHY

The Victoria History of the County of Hertford, edited by William Page, F.S.A., four volumes, with separate index, 1902-14.

History of Hertfordshire, John Edwin Cussans, three volumes, 1870-81.

History and Antiquities of Hertfordshire, Robert Clutterbuck, F.S.A., three volumes, 1815-27.

The Historical Antiquities of Hertfordshire, Sir Henry Chauncy, 1700. Reprinted and republished in two volumes, 1826.

The History of Hertfordshire, describing the County and its Ancient Monuments, Nathaniel Salmon, LL.B., 1728.

The History of the Abbey of St. Albans from the Founding thereof to its Dissolution (*with Lives of the Abbots*), Rev. Peter Newcome, rector of Shenley, 1795.

History of Hertford, Lewis Turnor, one volume, 1830.

Hertfordshire, Arthur Mee, revised edition by E. T. Long, with illustrations by A. F. Kersting, 1965.

Companion into Hertfordshire, W. Branch Johnson, 1952.

Hertfordshire, Sir William Beach Thomas, 1950.